POSITIVE
PSYCHOLOGY
THE **4** PILLARS OF HAPPINESS

How to Transform Your Life with Proven Strategies for Joy,
Confidence, and Emotional Resilience.
Unlock Your Full Potential and Conquer Your Fears

DAVID HEIMBACHER

Table of Contents

Foreword

Every day there is something new to do. Tasks, assignments, errands and other obligations fill the limited time available to you. It is easy to forget who actually plays the main role in your life: you! You are the most important thing in your life, because without you your life would not be possible. It is important not to completely lose attention to yourself. You must pay attention to yourself and you may make sure that you are happy. But how can you do that? Positive psychology, which you will learn about and use in this book, will help you.

First of all, it should be about your happiness: To do this, you'll first get a rough overview of what positive psychology is all about, learn what approaches are taken - and then you'll apply it all to yourself. The big goal is to increase your happiness and well-being. This topic extends to interpersonal relationships, which are also of great importance in this regard.

Next, you will receive a guide to positively influence other people. Impulses on argumentation, your personality and social interactions will help you to master interpersonal situations more easily and also to be able to influence people. The third chapter will deal with your emotions, which are essential for your personal development. Extensive knowledge about emotions and their effects will enable you to direct your emotions and use them for your own benefit.

Finally, toxic cycles will be dealt with: You will be given knowledge and methods to identify, analyze and break out of them. This will not only help you in the area of your social relationships, but will also have a positive impact on your emotions and self-image.

This book will give you a lot of knowledge, but also this realization: You are important! That's why you deserve to take care of yourself and develop.

Introduction

In ancient times, people have already philosophized about what a good life looks like. New currents of philosophy and different approaches to what constitutes happiness emerged. In modern times, there is a concrete science for this: positive psychology.

The science of psychology is not known for looking at personal happiness in people's lives. Rather, classical psychology deals with mental illnesses or disorders – that is, what is bad for people. After many years of focusing exclusively on the bad, it's now time to tackle the positive: Positive Psychology also has the potential to help you improve your life by increasing your happiness, satisfaction, self-confidence, and overall joy in living. A band-aid is not what you need to heal, but a light that shows you your strengths and happiness.

Even if you haven't actively engaged with psychology before, it's not an entirely unfamiliar field. You encounter it every day

- whether you're shopping in a supermarket, seeing an advertisement banner on your way to work, or being approached by a salesperson in a store. Every company strives to present itself in the best possible light and naturally employs psychological tactics to achieve this goal. Whether you're aware of it or not, you're constantly being influenced from the outside. Positive psychology can not only empower you to live a better life, but also enable you to identify your true desires and recognize when you're being influenced. You deserve to take control of your life without manipulation.

Each individual has their own life with unique challenges and opportunities, and everyone deserves the opportunity to overcome these challenges and seize opportunities. This is where positive psychology comes in because every person desires happiness.

How much potential lies within your life? With the help of new insights and methods, you can work on unleashing your full potential. Take an active role in your personal growth and initiate changes that will drastically improve your life!

First Pillar:
Positive Psychology and Your Well-Being

Recall a moment of pure happiness in your life. Perhaps it was when you found out you had landed your dream job or when you discovered you were expecting a child. It could have been after reaching a significant milestone or achieving a remarkable success. In that moment, you experienced a genuine and profound sense of happiness. True, this happiness doesn't last forever – that's a known fact. However, positive psychology teaches us that we can increase the amount of happiness and joy we feel on a daily basis.

What is Positive Psychology?

Positive psychology is a relatively new field within the larger discipline of psychology. Its central object of research: happiness. While classical psychology improves negatives, positive psychology directs its focus on the positive in order to further strengthen it. This shift from focusing on deficits to emphasizing available resources and their optimization has led to many insightful findings in the field. The knowledge gained from this field can aid in discovering greater happiness and satisfaction in life. It will provide support to help recognize and promote personal strengths, leading to overall personal growth. By applying positive psychology to every aspect of life, one can improve specific areas deemed important. In doing so, individuals can better themselves as a whole. (Müller, 2013, p. 5)

Positive psychology, however, isn't solely focused on happiness. The scope of positive psychology research is broad and has multiple interpretations. In 2005, positive psychology was defined by three pillars: positive emotions, character strengths, and institutions that nurture people, with the fourth pillar being relationships. In 2011, the four pillars were titled virtue, meaning, resilience, and well-being. This gives you an understanding of what positive psychology is and what it researches. Its aim is to aid individual development and strengthen positivity. By concentrating on positive aspects, such as strengths, success, or the ability to mentally resist, positive psychology can also help in preventing mental illnesses, such as depression. (Rolfe, 2019, pp. 17-18)

Now that you have gained knowledge in positive psychology, it's time to delve into the most extensive area of research and apply it to your personal happiness.

Your Well-Being

Not all happiness is the same, and there are different definitions of happiness. Two definitions are particularly relevant to you: Firstly, happiness is perceived as a favorable coincidence that arises when favorable circumstances come together. Secondly, happiness is a pleasant state characterized by joy and pleasure. If you are happy, you feel satisfied and in high spirits. (Duden, 2022c) The second definition is the one that will be focused on. There is also another term for this state: well-being. It refers to the state where an individual is doing well both physically and mentally. (Duden, 2022g) These two terms refer to the state that you strive to achieve: to be both physically and mentally healthy and happy.

Subjective Well-Being

In order to understand and enhance your personal well-being, it's crucial to acknowledge the existence of different types of well-being in psychology. Subjective well-being is particularly relevant, as happiness is a unique and personal experience for each individual. You have the power to define what happiness means to you because only you really know how you feel and when you are happy. When assessing your personal happiness, there are two parts to it: getting there and the results that follow. Positive life experiences lead to a sense of well-being. Initially, it's the ratio of good and bad emotions that determines your level of well-being. If you experience more positive emotions than negative, you are happier. Additionally, satisfaction with your life plays a significant role. This is divided into satisfaction with your life in general, i.e. an average of your life, and satisfaction with individual relevant areas. For example, if you are satisfied with all areas of your life except your work, then on average you will still be satisfied, but it won't feel that way to you because a very important part of your life doesn't yet meet your criteria for making you happy. Accordingly, you need to look not only at your life as a whole, but also at those parts of your life to which you give special importance. Finally, your view of your environment and life circumstances is also essential for subjective well-being. How do you perceive yourself? How do you evaluate yourself? How do you think about your circumstances, such as your material possessions, your social relationships, your job, etc.? How you perceive and evaluate this also contributes significantly to your subjective well-being. (Schmitz et al., 2018, pp. 2-3)

Example

You meet Mr. X on your way to work and he tells you about his life. He has a house and a daughter, a job he likes, and a wife he loves. You have a brief exchange with him about life and he starts to criticize his own. His house would be too small and he would like to have the roof replaced because the old roof doesn't look nice anymore. His daughter is going through a very stressful phase and it bothers him a lot that he has to constantly intervene and argue with her. Meanwhile, his wife has too little time for him because she also works and there is not much time left besides the child.

You have almost forgotten Mr. X, when you meet Mr. Y on the way back and can hardly believe how similar he is to Mr. X. You look almost the same and out of curiosity you talk to him. He too has a house and a daughter, a job he likes, and a wife he loves. You are amazed at how similar they are and ask him if there is anything that bothers him about his life. And he says, „Oh, you know, I have a lot of little problems in life, but they're not so bad. My roof is less beautiful than before, but I'm still happy because I chose the color myself and I still want to see it every day. My daughter is a bit of a handful right now, but every night when I see her go to sleep, it's worth every effort again to spend time with her. And my wife hasn't had much time for me in the last few weeks, but every evening we tell each other what we've been up to during the day and all the good things that have happened. I wouldn't say I have a perfect life, but I'm very happy with what I have."

In the example, you can see how the evaluation of one's own life circumstances plays a role in subjective well-being and satisfaction. But this is not only subjective – science has also found out a lot about it. That's why we're now talking about well-being in the psychological sense. (Ibid. p. 3)

Psychological Well-Being

Psychological well-being encompasses theoretical concepts beyond the aspects of subjective well-being. Basically it consists of six components: self-acceptance, self-determination, positive social relationships, active engagement with one's life circumstances, meaning, and growth. Each of these parts is important for psychological well-being. Self-acceptance goes beyond merely acknowledging oneself. It involves maintaining a positive outlook and developing affirming thoughts about oneself. Positive social relationships, which will be discussed further in the subsequent chapter, also play a critical role in nurturing psychological well-being. Actively shaping your own living conditions means that you are free to choose and shape your environment. In this context, meaning and purpose in life are philosophical constructs that contribute significantly to psychological well-being. Growth, on the other hand, is precisely what you are doing right now. It means recognizing your own potential, developing it, and growing from it. Finally, self-determination enables individuals to live according to their values.

Values are also an integral part of the journey towards discovering oneself. A value is something that one desires and strives for, based on their own principles, rather than being influenced by social norms. There is also not just one value in your life, but usually several values that serve as a guiding compass towards self-realization and personal growth. (Frey, 2016, p. 2)

Well-Being and Value Happiness

There isn't just one form of happiness. For instance, after a satisfying meal, you may feel happy. Similarly, you may feel happy when you've accomplished something significant. Of course, you are aware that these two feelings are not the same. This is where feel-good happiness and value happiness diverge. Feel-good happiness occurs when you engage in an activity that produces an immediate sense of happiness, such as eating good food or celebrating a triumph. This type of happiness is characterized by numerous positive emotions and an absence of negative emotions. On the other hand, value happiness is experienced when you engage in an activity that is personally important to you, such as personal growth or anything that adds significance to your life. Once again, values and meaning play crucial roles. To cultivate value happiness in your life, you can participate in activities that hold greater significance or meaning for you.

Example

Imagine living a whole day only according to what makes you immediately happy. You sleep very late because you feel good in bed, and you don't go to work because you find it exhausting. You watch a lot of TV and order food because cooking is not fun for you. You meet friends and go to a bar with them and drink as much as you want. On that day you felt very good, but on a long term you will not be happy with this way of life and you will not be able to continue it for a long time. On the other hand, a day of yours could also look like this:

You get up early and exercise because you've resolved to build more muscle and get fitter. Then you eat a breakfast that fits perfectly into your diet plan but you don't like it. You go to work and stay there all day because you earn so much money. In the evening, you occupy yourself with a book, which helps you educate yourself even more, and eventually retire early to bed, knowing that the following day will be just like today. However, this lifestyle will not make you happy either, because although you you may occasionally experience value happiness after achieving a goal, the daily feel-good happiness has entirely vanished from your life.

Accordingly, it is important that you have a healthy balance of wellbeing happiness and values happiness in your life.

Strategies to Increase Your Happiness and Well-Being

Now that you have acquired significant theoretical knowledge about happiness and well-being, you will now be taught practical methods to enhance these aspects in your life. It is important to note, however, that adopting one or two of these methods does not guarantee immediate happiness. Well-being is a deeply ingrained quality of life that requires more than, for example, smiling at least once a day.

What is the first thing you can do to feel better? It's to experience nature. The best way to do this is to go for a walk without any distractions. This includes talking to other people, music, or your smartphone. When you're not distracted, you can focus better on what's happening around you and take it in fully. Going for a walk is very effective because it gets you moving. Exercise has many benefits: it helps you relax, reduces stress, and supports mental processes. You will also have these benefits if you get into the habit of living more in the present. To do this, you can do something every day that you really enjoy. This can be a hobby, like drawing or playing an instrument, or spending time with a loved one, or taking your pet for a walk. It's about feeling good both physically and mentally. Your body's well-being includes your diet, which is why eating healthy and getting a healthy amount of sleep is also beneficial to your well-being. On the other hand, you can promote your mental well-being by getting to know yourself and other people better. You get to know yourself better by looking at your values and trying to live more by them. When you actively integrate your values into your life, you will notice that you are more energetic, satisfied, and fulfilled because you are living in harmony with yourself and your needs. However, other people also have a significant impact on your well-being. When you show appreciation to someone, they are more likely to reciprocate. That's why it makes a lot of difference to smile at a stranger on your way to work, to praise a colleague or to thank someone. Most of the (free) time you spend with other people, however, are with your friends, family, and partners around you. These close relationships, if they are good ones, benefit your emotional and physical well-being. In contrast, you should avoid those people who drain your energy. (Merkle & Wolf, 2019, pp. 212-215)

Properties that Promote Your Well-Being

There are not only methods that you can use for more well-being. There are also certain characteristics that can specifically help you experience more happiness and well-being.

Humor for More Happiness in Life

What do you associate humor with? Maybe you think of someone you know who always makes you laugh, or you think of famous comedians who make their living entertaining people. In fact, humor is not only associated with laughter, it is also the „ability and willingness to react cheerfully and calmly to certain things" (Duden, 2022e). Humor is a way of responding to a situation that was unexpected for you. However, since you always expect something from a situation, it depends on how big the difference is between what you expected as well as what really happened. Your reaction then depends on this difference. If you react with humor, it is easier for you to accept these events and not let them upset you. Scientifically, humor has many benefits because it causes people to laugh. For example, it has been shown that laughter releases tension - both physical and mental - and blocks thinking. Thus, it has an effective effect against anxiety, frustration, despair, and stress. This is due to the fact that laughter brings more oxygen into the bloodstream for a short period of time and increases the pulse, which in turn strengthens the cardiovascular system. Furthermore, the hormones serotonin and endorphins, also known as happiness hormones, are released in the brain. (Hagedorn, 2013, p. 78-79)

Example

You want to present your new project in a meeting, but none of your technical devices seem to work. The beamer doesn't focus properly and the presentation has hung up on your laptop. You feel yourself panicking - this presentation was supposed to be really good. But you notice that you're stressing out - you take a deep breath and say to your colleagues, „The project is definitely going better than the technology today." To this you grin and get a laugh back from a few colleagues. Immediately, the situation relaxes and you can turn more calmly to the technical problem. You restart your presentation, adjust the settings on the beamer, and then give the presentation exactly as you had imagined.

Another advantage of humor is that it promotes social bonds. This also has a significant impact on your well-being, because relationships are vital for everyone. The advantage is that laughter is a very strong social gesture that makes it easier to communicate with each other. This can be observed particularly well in the workplace where humor allows individuals of different levels to communicate with each other on the same level, without risking a loss of authority. This also has a positive impact on the sense of unity, as within a group, insider jokes tend to emerge - jokes that are based on knowledge that only members of the group possess. These particularly promote togetherness because these jokes seal off the group as a whole from outsiders, which strengthens the sense of the collective. Humor is also beneficial for people who are new to a group, as it helps facilitate social interactions. When people laugh together, they feel a sense of belonging, making it easier for new members to be perceived as part of the group. (Ibid. p. 79-80)

Example

It's your first day at your new workplace. All morning, a colleague has shown you around and shown you how everything works. Now it's break time and you join your colleagues in the common room. They are standing in a circle by the coffee machine and are talking about soccer because there was a game on last night. You were watching it, of course, so you can easily join in and laugh at your colleagues' jokes. Immediately, you feel better integrated than before. Now it is also no problem for you to seek direct conversation with new colleagues to ask them a question.

Humor also has personal benefits for you that go beyond your well-being. By releases tension, humor can open up new perspectives more quickly, making you more creative. Humor also affects how you evaluate situations. When a situation arises that you did not expect, you are more likely to view it as a challenge or a new opportunity, rather than developing a fear of risk. Lastly, humor also helps you reduce your stress levels. It's common to feel a lot of stress at work, especially when triggered by constant competition or a heavy workload. This stress can quickly damage your health by affecting your muscles, immune system, blood pressure, and other areas of your body. Humor, however, has the opposite effect - the positive hormones released relax the body and reduce any effects of stress. (Ibid. p. 82)

Now, to integrate more humor into your life, you should start with awareness. It always starts with a situation that you are not expecting. When you notice stress or panic building up inside you, you should choose to calm down and let go of those feelings, then reflect on what you did and should do in that situation. This will help you personally distance yourself from the situation and apply humor. By doing so, you interpret the absurdity of the situation not as dangerous, but as pleasant and an opportunity. (Ibid. p. 79)

Example

You have made an appointment with your supervisor to talk about your salary. Last week, you prepared intensively for this conversation but now your supervisor is late. You are worried that something has come up and that you will have to make another appointment, which will not be for several weeks... You get caught up into a thought spiral, but become aware of it. You take a breath and calm down. You decide to check your inbox to see if your supervisor has sent you an email. At that moment, your supervisor walks in and apologizes for being late. „No problem!," you say. „Your office was a nice change to check mail." You both laugh and then start the conversation. By choosing humor here, you've made the situation work for you and initiated a good start to the conversation.

Setting the Boundary Where It Counts - Resilience

Resilience starts when negative emotions occur. Being resilient means being psychologically resistant, and this trait can be trained as it is a variable in your life. Resilience greatly impacts your mental health, which is the foundation of your overall well-being. Two different types of factors contribute to resilience: risk factors and protective factors. Risk factors promote various diseases and have a negative impact on your well-being. Examples of risk factors include susceptibility to stress or poor self-regulation, as well as factors outside of your control, such as low levels of education among parents, low socioeconomic status, or poor living environments. These factors are counteracted by protective factors, which can be personal or social resources. All social resources have to do with your environment. These include stable relationships in your family that have fostered good communication and cohesion, good relationships with your siblings, and also good relationships with friends and partners. Personal resources, on the other hand, are characteristics that you can influence to become more resilient. While some factors, such as gender or intellectual abilities, are beyond your control, you can still influence how you perceive yourself, how you control yourself, and how you interact with others. Your sphere of influence also includes your problem-solving strategies and stress management techniques. (Helmin et al., 2019, pp. 68-69)

Example

According to a recent report that your boss has received, your department's performance has declined in the past few weeks. As a result, your boss has approached you and your colleagues to express his concerns and provide guidance on how to improve. While his lecture focused on the importance of work and the need to increase productivity, you couldn't help but take the criticism personally. The weight of his words stayed with you throughout the day and it became a constant distraction while you tried to focus on your work. Finally, you talk to a colleague who has also heard the criticism. He asks you, „Why are you taking this to heart?" You explain to him how you feel. „But it's not you. You're working as hard and as well as you can. There's no way these accusations apply to you alone." You ask your colleague why he is doing so well with this criticism, to which he replies, „I know that I work well and have no influence on how our colleagues work. If the boss criticized me personally, I would try to change something. But I simply don't have the influence to make each of our colleagues more productive. And because it's not up to me alone, I don't have to beat myself up about it."

In this example, you can observe how your colleague handles a situation differently due to his resilience and reaps significant benefits from it. As a result, he is more at ease, can concentrate on his own work, and is therefore more productive. If you aim to acquire these same advantages, it is worthwhile to explore how you can cultivate more resilience in yourself. This is precisely what the following discussion entails.

To build your resilience, you can cultivate these qualities. You can observe your social life and pay attention to how you interact with people close to you. You can pay attention to how you think about yourself and counter negative thoughts directly with positive ones. Additionally, there are practical exercises you can do to become more resilient. The first exercise is to identify your individual strengths, and there are several methods you can use for this. You can take self-tests or create a list of qualities that you perceive as strengths in yourself. Another effective method is to ask people close to you for their input since they can provide valuable insights into your strengths that you may not have considered. Another strategy that promotes resilience is is to maintain a diary where you record successes and moments of happiness. By jotting down your achievements and happy moments each day, you can create a collection of positive experiences that you can refer to whenever you need to boost your mood. This exercise also motivates you to intentionally seek out new successes and moments of joy to add to your diary. Of course, there are not only exercises that promote the positive, but also those that mitigate the negative. For instance, you can make a list of things that are currently causing stress in your life and identify individual measures to manage them effectively. (Ibid. p. 70-71)

Example

One evening, you arrive home feeling completely overwhelmed and decide that you can no longer handle the level of stress in your life. You take stock of the various stressors in your life and identify two major factors causing the most stress: your work, where you have an excessive workload and insufficient time to complete it, and your girlfriend, who expects you to be available for spontaneous hangouts. You create two separate lists, one for each stress factor, and brainstorm potential actions to reduce stress in the future. For your work-related stress, you have decided to be more assertive and communicate with your boss when you have too much on your plate. Additionally, you want to minimize distractions to increase your productivity. For your girlfriend-related stress, you plan to have an honest conversation with her and let her know that you can't always be available to her. You also intend to prioritize your time between her and yourself.

You will now implement these measures and evaluate their effectiveness in reducing your stress levels. If successful, you will continue to use the same measures, otherwise, you will seek alternative solutions and repeat the cycle.

You may now have an understanding of which characteristics can contribute to your happiness, but their relevance lies in their application. Humor can help foster connections with others, while resilience can help protect you from negative experiences. These qualities are especially important in relationships, as it is through them that you can truly utilize your strengths. Let's now discuss relationships and how these qualities can play a role in building and maintaining them.

Self-Esteem and Acceptance

Self-esteem is a valuable quality that stems from accepting yourself as you are. However, if you feel that you lack self-confidence and self-esteem, it may be due to your upbringing in your childhood. During the early years of your life, you learn from your parents and adopt their beliefs, criticisms, and evaluations. Any negative experiences or feelings of devaluation that you experienced during childhood can persist into adulthood and affect your self-esteem. (Merkle & Wolf, 2019, pp. 54-56)

If you're working on improving your self-esteem, you'll likely face challenging situations that require you to overcome them. These exercises will help you grow the most, so it's worth it to persevere. To improve your self-esteem, start by avoiding negative self-talk. Don't use insulting terms or adjectives like „stupid," „hopeless," or „failure" to describe yourself. Accept that you're not perfect, and stop criticizing yourself all the time. You'll find that you begin to value yourself more. You should also start separating who you are from what you do. If you make a mistake, you're not a bad person. Don't question yourself just because you've done something wrong. Instead of always criticizing yourself, highlight what you are good at and what you enjoy doing. Think about your successes and praise yourself for them. A simple physical exercise you can do is to make two lists. First, write down the things that you criticize yourself for. Then, challenge those criticisms by finding positive qualities in them. Do you constantly criticize yourself for being impatient? Then, in reality, you just have a lot of energy and drive. Next, for your self-esteem, make a list of the things you like about yourself. What qualities do you find remarkable, or what do others often compliment you on? Perhaps you are particularly tidy or always have an open ear for those around you. You can refer back to this list when you need a boost. Last, don't compare yourself, either to other people or to the person you want to be. The ideal image you have of yourself is created from expectations and perceptions you have experienced over your lifetime. Instead of using this ideal image as a standard, find your own ideals and try to develop in that direction. Comparing yourself to others doesn't help your self-esteem either, as you are an individual with unique strengths and weaknesses. Instead, focus on your own progress and be proud of what you've achieved! (Ibid. p. 63-68)

Your Relations

You already know that good relationships have a big impact on your well-being. To foster them, it's important to focus on improving your approach toward them. The following text will show you how you can build, find, and maintain positive relationships.

New Relationship: How to Win Sympathy

To rebuild a relationship, it's crucial to start on the right foot. Everything starts when you meet a person for the first time. This doesn't necessarily have to be the very first time you meet them, but rather the first meeting within a day or a week. However, the very first encounter can have the greatest impact. It is very simple – smile! We are not talking about a quick nod or a humorous grin, but a real smile. This shows that you are friendly and open-minded, leaving a positive and lasting first impression. Even when you don't feel like smiling, forcing yourself to do so and thinking of something positive can make a world of difference. This is because your inner state, not external circumstances, determines how you feel. Furthermore, your feelings and behavior are directly related, one influencing the other. So, by forcing yourself to smile, you can improve your overall mood (Carnegie, 2019, pp. 101-102).

When you meet someone for the first time, smile, and introduce yourself by name. Remembering a person's name is essential, as each person's name holds a special meaning for them. During conversations, use their name, as it acts as a compliment and shows that you're attentive, leaving a positive impression. You meet several people every day, making it difficult to remember everyone's names. However, it can be made easier by finding out a few details about the person, such as their work, hobbies, interests, or relationship status. You don't need to remember all the details, but rather the name, along with one or two bullet points. The next time you meet, you can bring up the name and topic of conversation, making the interaction more comfortable and memorable (Ibid. pp. 107-108).

Example

You're attending a party organized by your company, and you arrived there alone. While talking to a few colleagues, another colleague introduces their husband. You immediately smile and pay attention as he introduces himself. As the conversation progresses, you continue to engage with him, and later when you meet him again, you address him by his name, Mr. X. After chatting for a few minutes, you discover that Mr. X works for a different company in the HR department, and they have recently advertised a new job. Coincidentally, you happen to know someone who would be the perfect fit for the job. You share your contact information with Mr. X, and in doing so, you have done a favor for both Mr. X and your acquaintance.

This example highlights the significant impact that a smile and remembering a person's name can have. However, it's essential to continue the conversation by demonstrating genuine interest in the other person. Not only does this help you to remember their name, as previously mentioned, but it also indicates to them that you value their presence. Have you ever noticed that people tend to talk about themselves in most conversations? It's a natural human tendency. So, if you share an interest in the person's life, they will naturally appreciate your company. (Ibid. p. 84) To show a sincere interest, ask the person questions about their life, such as their hobbies, interests, or things that are important to them. If they mention something they are passionate about, dive deeper and ask more about it. They will be delighted to share their enthusiasm with someone who is genuinely interested in what they have to say. (Ibid. pp. 127-128)

If you are truly interested in what another person is saying, they will perceive you as friendly, open, and sympathetic. However, merely asking a question and then diverting your attention to something else while your conversation partner speaks is not enough. You need to actively listen with attentiveness. There are various listening techniques you can use in different situations to achieve this.

Different Types of Listening and Their Benefits

If you ask someone a question, they may respond without organizing their thoughts beforehand. As a result, neither you nor the person you're speaking with will know what the final outcome of the conversation will be. In such situations, it's best to use receptive listening techniques. You should listen patiently to the other person without interrupting them. You can maintain eye contact, but avoid doing so for too long, as prolonged eye contact can be just as distracting as interruptions. Show that you're paying attention without interjecting your own thoughts. By doing so, the other person will have the space to think about what they want to say on their own, and the conversation will move in the direction they prefer. All you need to do is be reserved, attentive, and focused. (Preuß-Scheuerle, 2016, pp. 24-25)

Example

You were asked to meet with your boss to discuss a report you recently wrote. However, you were confident that you had done a good job. As soon as you sat in your boss's office and he began speaking, you realized that the meeting was not entirely about the report. Rather than interrupting or trying to steer the conversation, you decided to simply listen and let your boss speak. „In summary, your report was really good, but I didn't like a couple of metrics. Although, of course, it is an accurate representation of the project. But that would mean that the project is going exactly according to plan. I think you should allow a buffer of about two days in the project though. Exactly, the project should be further along, but it is not. Your report shows that very clearly - so look to move the project along a little faster so that you have buffer at the end to be able to incorporate final changes if you need to."

By allowing your boss to speak without interruption, you were able to better understand his feedback and concerns. You took yourself back and found out in the end what the problem really was.

However, not every conversation is simple or clear. You may have experienced a situation where a misunderstanding arises so quickly that you wish to end the conversation. In such situations, paraphrased listening can be helpful. This involves repeating what has been said in your own words to ensure that you fully understand your counterpart's message. Additionally, if you have misunderstood something, your counterpart can correct you directly. This way of listening will make your communication more efficient and clearer, and you will show your interlocutor that you under-stand what he wants from you. In doing so, you must be careful not to interpret what is being said and not to be influenced by your own opinion - because if you constantly misrepresent what has been said, it can upset other people. In conversations that can quickly degenerate into conflict, this kind of listening is very helpful because repeating and rephrasing gives you time to calm down and get your feelings under control. (Ibid. pp. 25-27)

Example

You have agreed to take on a task for a colleague, but unfor-tunately, they did not explain the task well. Their explanation lacked structure, and they often get muddled in their sentences while speaking.

Colleague: "So the plan has to be ready first, but - wait - you also have to notify the other colleagues. I think part of it also has to be agreed with another colleague - but I don't know which one of them. Probably from the other department."

You: "So if I understand correctly, my first step is to complete the plan. Next, I will need to review it with a colleague from the other department to get their approval. Then, I will send the plan to the colleagues involved in the project, right?"

Colleague: „Yes, exactly!"

Your colleague confirmed your understanding of the task, and now you have a clear understanding of what you need to do. Despite your colleague's inability to explain the task well, your paraphrasing helped you understand and start the task more quickly.

The last method is active listening, which is particularly suitable in conversations with a lot of tension. It helps everyone involved in the conversation to understand and trust each other. You pay attention not only to what is being said, but also to how the person feels about it and what they want. Look for underlying motivations, feelings, and interests. Accordingly, don't repeat what was said, but briefly summarize the contect as you understand it. This will make it easier for you to understand the other person's perspective and make the conversation's direction more productive. (Ibid. p. 28-29)

Example

You are sitting in a bar with your friend after work and he is talking about his job. You can tell that something is bothering him as he mentions having to spend a lot of time at work in the last few weeks.

You: „So you're stressed because you have to work so much?" Here, you try to summarize his emotional state.

Friend: "Yeah, the work is really taking a lot out of me right now. But I really like doing it, you know - I've wanted to have a job like this for so long. And now that it's getting busy, my girlfriend is constantly mad at me for spending so much time at work."

Your friend feels understood and continues to open up about what is really bothering him: his girlfriend.

You: „Oh, so work is fine, but your girlfriend is stressing you out?" You keep trying to summarize how he feels.

Friend: „Exactly! Yet she knows exactly how important work is. And it's not like she never stays too long at her job."

By actively listening, you were able to identify the real problem and can now give your friend appropriate advice.

Existing Relationships – How to Find and Maintain the Right Relationships

Of course, you don't need to rebuild every relationship in your life, as you already have established connections with various individuals, such as family members, friends, partners, and even acquaintances. To discover these existing positive relationships, you can conduct an exercise by reviewing your contact list. While traditional address books can still be used, the more prevalent option today is the directory of contacts on your smartphone. Go through your list of contacts and identify individuals who are genuine connections. These are people who know you well, with whom you can have fun or share your sorrows, or simply be in each other's company. When you find these people, , make concrete plans to meet them in person, as an email or message may not suffice. Real contact brings people together, something that a message cannot achieve. (Blickhan, 2015, p. 261)

Once you have established a relationship with someone, it is important to nurture it in order to maintain it. Communication between two individuals plays a significant role in the stability of the relationship. If negative statements outweigh the positive ones, the relationship is likely to end sooner or later. However, a positive and meaningful relationship requires more than just a good ratio of positive to negative statements. It involves both parties being kind to each other, acknowledging each other, and showing respect and appreciation for one another's lives. This includes sharing beautiful moments together, actively planning activities that can bring joy, and recreating past positive experiences by talking about them. In any type of relationship, whether it is familial, platonic, or romantic, both individuals need to turn to each other. This means paying attention to each other, showing interest in each other's lives, and actively listening to each other. Perhaps you once knew someone who never listened to you and only talked about themselves. Were you very fond of this person? Certainly not, because this communication was not constructive, but rather destructive. It is essential to avoid destructive communication, which can be categorized as active or passive. Active destructive communication involves devaluing the other person, while passive destructive communication involves minimizing contact to the point that the other person feels ignored. When a person communicates with you in a passively destructive way, he or she will devalue your feelings, question your views, and portray himself or herself as more powerful than you. Passively destructive communication is just as damaging, because here another person makes you think they don't take you seriously or even notice you. Constructive communication, on the other hand, involves paying attention to the other person's thoughts and feelings and allowing them the space to express themselves. (Ibid. pp. 261-264)

Example

You meet a friend at a café, coincidentally, he happens to be in town and wanted to catch up with you. After discussing his work for a while, you mention that you are currently managing an important project that you consider to be a promising opportunity. However, your friend sees it differently. „Hmm, that doesn't sound so promising to me. And do you think you're up to managing a project like that Even though you are confident in your abilities, his doubts make you uncertain.

„We can catch up again next time then you can tell us then how it went. I'm sure we'll see each other again soon." Within minutes, the conversation is over, and your friend is gone. You are now not only unsure but also feel like your friend doesn't take you seriously. You decide not to meet with him again next time.

In this example, you first learned about actively destructive communication, followed by passively destructive communication. If you notice that people around you often communicate destructively, it should serve as a warning signal, and you should reconsider your relationship with them.

However, not every relationship is destructive, and many can have a positive impact on your life. You already know that a good relationship requires kindness, appreciation, and constructive communication. Now, let's talk about having a generally positive attitude.

Assuming that a person wants to harm you fundamentally cannot result in a good relationship. On the other hand, if you first assume positive things about a person, you can establish a relationship. The same applies to criticism. When you criticize someone, be careful not to devalue them as individuals, but only to address the behavior that was not acceptable. Criticism is a natural part of any relationship because conflicts can arise between two people. It's essential to resolve such conflicts before they escalate into a loud argument. Strategies to resolve conflicts include active listening, which you'll learn about in a later chapter. (Ibid. p. 264)

Summary

In the first chapter, you learned about positive psychology, which focuses on positive emotions, character strengths, and institutions that support individuals. At the center of this field is well-being, which has several types, such as subjective well-being, where personal perception plays a significant role. Psychological well-being, on the other hand, is an interplay of self-acceptance, self-determination, relationships, impact on one's life, meaning, and growth. It's essential to distinguish between value happiness and well-being happiness. The latter refers to the immediate feeling of making yourself happy, such as by eating well, while value happiness is the sense of importance in your life.

Humor and resilience are qualities that promote well-being and can be cultivated to increase happiness. These qualities also have a significant impact on your relationships, which play a crucial role in your overall well-being. When starting a new relationship, it's important to make a likable first impression, show interest in the other person, and actively listen. In existing positive relationships, it's crucial to maintain real contact and take good care of them. Constructive communication is beneficial, while destructive communication can cause significant damage to any relationship. Therefore, it's important to pay attention to your communication style.

Second Pillar:
Influencing People Positively

You now know a lot about positive psychology, happiness, and well-being. But it's important that you take the right steps to achieve more happiness. There will be many obstacles in your way, including the people around you. This chapter is about positively influencing and persuading people. The point is not to manipulate anyone but to show other points of view and make people think.

But what does it mean to persuade? A person can tell you that they like your approaches and support your opinion, but that doesn't necessarily mean they will do what you say. There are four aspects to real persuasion. The first is understanding: your counterpart must understand exactly what you are talking about. You must, therefore, be careful not to use too many complex technical terms and explain complicated issues in a simple and understandable way. Next comes your credibility: This is where your charisma is called for. Next comes your credibility: this is where your charisma is called for. You must show that you are convinced that what you are saying is correct and important. If you are not convinced or don't show it enough, the other person will notice and not believe you. Next, it takes understanding in the other direction: your conversation partner needs to realize that it's about them. You have to make them feel that their interests and needs are being addressed. To do this, show them that you understand them and know what they're interested in. Here you can also address any problems in his life to show that you really know what makes him tick Here, you can also address any problems in their life to show that you really know what makes them tick. Lastly, it's about selling your content. After you have built trust between you and your counterpart, they also need to see that your idea is valuable to them. If they accept your idea for themselves, you have successfully convinced them. (Prost, 2010, p. 80)

How to Convince People – Some Basic Rules

Before delving into methods such as argumentation or intensive work on your personality, you will learn basic rules to follow when trying to convince someone of something. The first and foremost rule is to avoid arguing with your counterpart at all costs. The best way to do this is to withhold your initial reaction and contemplate whether you genuinely want to respond in that manner. Typically, the first response is impulsive and loaded with emotions, which is why it can easily lead to an argument. However, you're not looking to defend yourself; you're aiming for a discussion. Therefore, you must be able to regulate your temper. The most effective way to steer clear of an argument is as follows: respond to your counterpart, listen attentively, and defer significant decisions. By doing so, you prioritize your relationship with the other person and demonstrate that you can act rationally. (Carnegie, 2019, pp. 157-158)

Just as you must pay attention to your counterpart in a conflict, you must also do the same in other situations. If you want to convince someone, you must always remember that you are dealing with a person who has personality and pride. Therefore, you should never hurt your counterpart's honor and always remain friendly! If you have said something wrong, admit it. This shows courtesy and goodwill. Additionally, you should listen to what your counterpart says because it is possible that you are wrong. Even if you disagree, you should show that you are considering their point of view. If you demonstrate that you are willing to compromise, most people will reciprocate and accommodate you. (Ibid. p. 242)

However, there are also some useful tips that can take you a few steps further in a conversation, and you should know them as well. First, you need to ensure that your counterpart says "yes" as often as possible. This creates the impression that they agree with you in general, even though they might only agree with specific questions. Additionally, try to take up as little space in the conversation as possible and let the other person speak. You can still ask questions to which the other person will answer „yes," but otherwise, let them speak. In many cases, they will convince themselves, and you will not have to do much more. Another way to steer the conversation is to give your counterpart the impression that the idea, which actually came from you, came from them. If you can convincingly convey this impression, your counterpart will have to support the idea to save face. Why? Simply put, no one submits an idea and then turns against it – that would be contradictory. If all else fails, you have two options. The first is to appeal to the person's noble sentiment, invoking higher values that society likes to see. Alternatively, you can challenge the person to a competition to convince you of their cause. People are naturally competitive and seek recognition from others, so you can use that to your advantage. (Ibid.)

Ultimate Persuasion - What You Need to Know about Argumentation

In order to persuade someone, it is crucial to present strong arguments. The initial step involves crafting the content: your arguments should be accurate in terms of facts and must be organized in a logical manner. For instance, if you're discussing a sequence of events, chronological arguments would be more effective than presenting advantages and disadvantages.

Example

You're at work with some colleagues and considering going to a bar together in the evening. However, one of your colleagues is hesitant because they have an important meeting with a client the next day and need to be fully prepared. Nevertheless, you want them to join in on the fun.

Argument 1: „I get that you want to be in good shape tomorrow, but it's really more fun when you're there!"

Argument 2: „Your presentation isn't until lunchtime, so you could come and just leave early if that's convenient for you. It's really important to me to have you there."

The first argument does not seem convincing here, because it does not address your colleague's concerns, focuses on the enjoyment of the group as a whole. Your second argument, on the other hand, addresses your colleague's needs while still emphasizing the importance of their presence to you.

Structure Your Argumentation

An important part of an argument is structure. It helps you communicate more effectively by making your argument more effective and easier to follow. The simplest structures have three parts, which include an introduction, a body, and a conclusion. In the introduction, you provide context for the argument. What is the current situation? Why is this particular topic relevant? Then in the main body, you present your argument and reasoning. Give reasons for your argument and how you arrived at your conclusion. In the conclusion, you offer a suggestion on how to proceed afterwards. You are asking someone to consider your argument and act accordingly. (Preuß-Scheuerle, 2016, p. 45)

Example

You are discussing with your boss the possibility of involving another colleague in a project that you are currently managing. While you are in favor of this idea, your boss believes that the colleague is needed in their department.

You: „Our project has been around for a while, and we've invested a lot of money in it as a company. As it has grown, we now have more work to do, and we need more support to handle it. I think Mr. X would be an excellent addition to the project, and he could contribute more to it than he currently does in his own department. That's why I want him to be involved."

This argument structure involves summarizing and revisiting the issue, providing a reason, and requesting action from your boss. It is clear, understandable, and very convincing.

Argumentation structures are useful when dealing with complex topics. If a three-step structure is not enough, you can easily add more steps to a familiar structure. In the example above, the Situation, Reason, and Call structure were used. It can be extended by adding another reason or explanation. If you are dealing with a very complex topic, using a multi-step argument structure allows you to thoroughly cover your topic without losing the thread or confusing your audience. A simple chain argument is an alternative to a structured argument that can be adapted to suit your needs in a given situation. The concept behind chain argumentation is that arguments build upon each other. It is best if the arguments support each other logically or chronologically. Chain reasoning is especially useful when you need to provide multiple arguments to support a view and also want to cite evidence to back them up. This approach makes your argument more compelling and effective. (Ibid. p. 48)

Example

You are in the final phase of a work project that you have invested a lot of time and energy into and are very proud of the results. One of your colleagues has not quite finished their task and would like to postpone the final presentation by a few days. However, you know that the majority of colleagues in the project are against this, and you first talk to the colleague personally to dissuade them.

You: „I don't think it would benefit the project as a whole if we postponed the presentation. We had good planning from the start, and always supported each other. We had regular updates and resolved issues promptly. Even as we approached the end, we still discussed what needed to be done. It's a problem that you didn't ask for support earlier, but now we should focus on the original plan and prepare the presentation for the scheduled day."

This argument uses the chronological sequence of steps in the project, which you link with arguments during the process. By doing so, you presented your colleague with several valid arguments that they could follow logically and chronologically. Alternatively, your arguments could have been logically related only:

You: „I am against postponing the presentation. Firstly, many good colleagues in this project are already involved in other things after the fixed date. Secondly, we have used a good structure to enable mutual support. We met often, sent out many updates, and made sure everyone got help when they needed it. It's a problem that you didn't ask for help earlier, but we've already planned the presentation and need to start preparing for it."

In this argument, you elaborate more on an argument, give a good rationale, and look at the next steps. This is also very convincing, as it shows that you can take several points of view and have thought about the further procedure.

What Types of Arguments You Can Use

When applying an argument structure, finding the arguments to support it can be difficult. However, you can make it easier by specifically looking for different types of arguments. One useful type of argument is the factual argument, which is based on proven facts such as figures or data from studies, research results, or evaluations. It is convincing because it cannot be doubted by your opponent. However, it is crucial that factual arguments are both correct and relevant to the discussion. Otherwise, they can quickly destroy your credibility. Another type of argument that is just as convincing as a factual argument is a normative argument, which is based on generally accepted norms or rules. Your interlocutors cannot challenge these because they are already widely known and accepted. As with factual arguments, it is important to use only relevant normative arguments. A rather difficult type of argument is the plausibility argument, but it is very convincing if used well. The plausibility argument is a rather difficult type of argument, but it can be very convincing if used well. It relies on logical connections that can be derived and explained clearly to everyone in the discussion. If others can understand your argument, it will be convincing. This type of argument is particularly suitable for simple conclusions. (Dr. Detlef Langermann, 2004, p. 11)

Example

During your lunch break, you are chatting with a friend about a colleague who wants to take unplanned leave even though he is currently needed in his department. While you think it's fine because you know some of the colleagues in the department and trust them, your friend disagrees, arguing that unplanned leave requires a lot of planning and would cause unnecessary hassle. To support your colleague, you present a factual argument: „He deserves the vacation because he has successfully completed three projects in the last four months, all of which have significantly benefited the company." Your friend cannot dispute these facts. Alternatively, you could use a normative argument: „He works tirelessly, and it's only fair that he gets some time off." This approach appeals to a generally accepted rule.

You can persuade people in different ways, including by involving other people. One effective method is using the authority argument, which is based on facts supported by known experts in a field, such as researchers, scientists, politicians, or authorities. Including these arguments at the end of your own argument can make it more convincing. Additionally, you can refer to external factors without mentioning other people by using a comparative argument. This involves comparing similar points and drawing conclusions about the topic at hand. It is more effective if your opponent is familiar with both points being compared. If your counterpart presents a particularly strong argument, consider using it to support your own position. This not only weakens the other side's argument but also indirectly strengthens your own. An indirect argument is highly persuasive because it demonstrates that your argument is well-thought-out and has solid support. You can also use indirect argumentation to show that you can respond well to new arguments on the fly. (Ibid.)

Example

You are discussing different cars with your partner because you want to buy a new vehicle together. As there is a lot of money involved, you are not yet in agreement about which model and brand you both prefer. You are in favor of a fast car that is easy to drive, while your partner would like to have a car with a lot of storage space and more than two seats for possible family growth. You argue that a larger car would use a lot more fuel and would not be worth it since the close involvement at work you both have means you don't want to plan a family yet. (Here, you argue indirectly by rebutting an argument made by your partner.) You tell of a colleague who bought a new car some time ago and was much happier with a sporty car. (Here, you cite authority because your colleague has experience with this topic.) You suggest comparing the two cars on the spot so that the conversation does not degenerate into an argument. On the spot, you can use the comparison to argue more strongly and emphasize the advantages of the car of your choice.

Now that you know about the different types of arguments and what to look for when preparing for a discussion, make sure to have as many different types of arguments ready as possible. Even if you don't need all of your arguments, having a variety of them at your disposal can help you persuade your audience more effectively.

How You Process Information

Persuading other people can also be understood from a psychological perspective. What distinguishes people in terms of how they are persuaded? The answer to that is how they process information. People have different ways of processing information, and paying attention to that can give you a significant advantage. You can typically identify a person's processing pattern by observing their reactions during a conversation. Once you have identified their leaning, you can adapt your arguments accordingly and be more successful in persuading them. (Preuß-Scheuerle, 2016, p. 51)

The concept of „gut feeling" is likely familiar to you. It refers to an emotional assessment that is not based on reason (Duden, 2022a), and many people rely on it when making decisions. This approach is essentially a way of processing information, with those who use it focusing on what their feelings tell them. If they feel comfortable with something, they are almost convinced to choose it. This group of people does not place much importance on the opinions of others. When dealing with individuals who make decisions based on their gut feeling, it's important to involve them in the decision-making process and ask for their personal opinion. This will give you insight into their stance on the matter and the concerns that still need to be addressed. To persuade this group of people, use suitable arguments such as factual, normative, and plausibility arguments that are easily comprehensible. However, it's important to avoid using the authority argument in discussions with this group. (Ibid. p. 52)

The second type of people is the opposite of those who listen to their own feelings. They pay attention to what others think and seek approval and likability from others. It's common to come across such individuals since many people value the opinions of others. To convince someone with this type of mindset, it's best to present multiple arguments that involve other people. You can compare the current situation with that of another person, and share experiences and opinions of others. Additionally, the authority argument can be effective since it not only presents an external perspective but also comes from a position of authority. (Ibid.)

Example

You have a meeting with your boss to discuss the possibility of hiring a new team member in your department. You strongly support the idea as it would alleviate the workload for you and your colleagues and increase productivity. However, you know that your boss tends to rely on his gut feeling rather than facts and figures. Therefore, you decide to approach the conversation in a way that aligns with his decision-making pattern. After some initial small talk, you ask your boss for his opinion on the current state of the department and its potential for improvement. You have some numbers and arguments to support your case, but you also make sure to involve your boss in the discussion. You explain that hiring another colleague would streamline project timelines, ultimately leading to increased productivity. Your boss is receptive to these arguments and agrees with you in the end.

On the other hand, you also need to discuss the matter with a colleague from HR whom you don't know very well. In the first few minutes of your conversation, you notice that he is someone who places a high value on others' opinions. So, you decide to present your case using this approach. You mention that many of your colleagues are in favor of the idea and that your boss has already agreed to it. This tactic proves to be effective as the colleague quickly comes around to your point of view, given the weight of other people's opinions in his decision-making process.

It's important to focus on the positive aspects and avoid talking about negative outcomes. In contrast, there's another type of person who tends to focus on the negative and thinks about what could go wrong. To convince this type of person, it's better to emphasize the potential negative consequences of not taking action. Highlight scenarios where people could get hurt or something could get damaged, and present different probabilities for each scenario. Comparisons that make the current situation look bad work particularly well with this type. (Ibid.)

Example

It continues with convincing people about hiring a new colleague. You thought the discussion was over, but then you learned through a colleague that the head of HR disagrees with you. Now, you need to talk to him to gain his support. Fortunately, you don't have to worry about how to convince him because it's widely known in the company that he is extremely goal-oriented and determined. So, you already know that you need to strongly emphasize the goal - more productivity and employee satisfaction.

You: „Mr. X, I heard that you disagree with my proposal to hire a new colleague. Firstly, I would like to apologize for not speaking to you in person earlier. I would be happy to briefly explain why I feel so strongly about my proposal. My department continues to deliver good work and is highly regarded within the company. However, we have been getting busier and busier for some time now and have less time to accomplish all the tasks. Another colleague would not only increase our department's productivity but also alleviate the workload of other colleagues, which would contribute to their satisfaction. We have several ideas to use this new person, and I believe it will contribute to the company's long-term success."

In this argument, you focused on emphasizing the positive outcomes that hiring a new colleague would bring. How would have this argument if you were speaking to someone who is more motivated by avoiding negative outcomes?

You: „Mr. X, I heard that you disagreed with my proposal to hire a new colleague. First of all, I would like to apologize for not having spoken to you in person earlier, but the situation at our company is stressful right now. Our department is highly regarded all over the company and the workload in our department has been increasing rapidly. Meanwhile, we lack the necessary staff to process all orders in a reasonable time. I can't imagine that this will go on much longer. Other colleagues are also complaining more and more that it's getting too much work and they'd like more support."

In this argument, you have effectively outlined the current issue. As your counterpart is aligned with your perspective, you have successfully convinced them.

You have learned about several patterns of how people process information and make decisions, but there are more that are relevant to consider. Another pattern is based on necessity, where individuals ask themselves what needs to happen and whether something is truly necessary. They prefer to stick with what they know and what they can be sure of, as this helps them maintain a stable and continuous environment, which is very important to them. To convince someone who falls into this category, you must demonstrate the necessity of your proposal. Provide compelling reasons and ensure that the person understands that what you are suggesting is truly important and necessary. An argumentation that highlights the interplay of cause and effect can help underscore the necessity of your proposal. Conversely, there is another pattern that centers around possibilities. These are those people who like to think about the future. These individuals are forward-thinking and like to consider what is still possible and what opportunities may arise. To persuade these people, you need to present them with vivid possibilities - doors that can be opened to move forward or potential opportunities that may emerge. To win over someone who falls into this category, you will need to present them with strong arguments and emphasize the potential of your proposal. (Ibid. pp. 52-53)

Example

You feel underutilized at work lately and have already talked about it with friends and colleagues. Now, you want to address your boss about it and take on more responsibility. You have known your boss for a long time and know that he always pays attention to whether something is really necessary - he decides according to necessity. So, during the conversation, you should emphasize the necessity of this decision for both yourself and the company.

You: „I would like to take on more responsibility within the company. I have proven myself several times over the years and I am ready for new challenges. Currently, I do not feel fully utilized in my professional capacity, and I am willing to explore other career options if necessary. „

Of course, you have no intention of quitting by any means, but the prospect of losing a good, qualified employee creates the kind of need your boss needs to make this decision. If your boss were part of the pattern that likes to see opportunities, your reasoning may look like this:

You: „I would like to take on more responsibility within the company. Over the years, I have gained a lot of experience and skills, and I believe that I can make a significant contribution to the success of the company. „

Here, you are presenting your boss with the prospect of contributing much more to the company. He now has an opportunity that he can seize, which is very convincing to him.

The last two patterns you should be aware of are the ones that focus on similarities and differences. The first type wants to see similarities, and looks for connections and commonalities. To persuade these people, you should also specifically look for similarities and highlight them. By pointing out similarities or commonalities, you can quickly win over this type. It's best to leave out anything that is objectionable or contrasting because that fits with the opposite pattern: those who look for differences. They want to be shown alternative perspectives and different points of view. During conversations, it helps to call for other opinions or positions to be expressed. Words such as „in contrast to" or „difference" are particularly welcome to this type and can strengthen your argumentation.

Example

You are preparing for two meetings in which you want to talk to two different colleagues about a new mailing list. The first colleague is known to prefer the old ways of doing things. You anticipate that he would be resistant to hearing about anything new. To persuade him, you collect some points about the new mailing list that are similar to an old list that he already knows and uses. You don't know the second colleague very well, but you've heard that he's very adventurous in the workplace and likes to take chances. You assess him as the type who is open to differences and seeks out opportunities. Therefore, you prepare some arguments that highlight the new opportunities and benefits that your mailing list would offer. In this case, it is important that you meet with each colleague independently and not have them sit together in a meeting. Trying to combine arguments that focus on similarities and differences can be challenging and may not convince both types of people.

Now that you have learned about the eight different patterns of how people process information, you may have thought of various individuals around you, including yourself. It is highly beneficial to identify which of these patterns applies to you. This way, you can look for specific ways to convince yourself of something, like a task that you've been procrastinating on. You can also recognize when someone is trying to persuade you. Ask yourself: Do I truly like the thing itself, or am I merely swayed by the arguments and how they are presented? How would I feel about it if there were other arguments presented or no arguments at all?

In Summary

People process information in different ways. Some are more introspective and respond best to good arguments presented without the input of others. Others are more socially-oriented, and care a great deal about what other people think. For these individuals, it's helpful to use comparisons and experiences of other people to make your case. There are also those who are more focused on achieving a certain outcome or avoiding a negative one. To persuade them, you can present the desired outcome in a positive light or highlight the negative aspects of the current situation. Some people make decisions based on necessity or opportunity, so it's important to demonstrate that your proposal is either necessary or has significant potential for improvement. The last two patterns decide according to similarities or differences. It's important to highlight the relevant similarities or differences and use language that resonates with them.

How to Convince Verbally and Non-Verbally

To effectively persuade someone, it's not only important to have good arguments but also to present them in the right framework. You convey an image of yourself to others through language, posture, action, and appearance, which they use to judge and decide whether or not to trust you. Therefore, if you present a good argument, you should also behave in a way that reinforces its validity. This is what we'll discuss now – your language and body language.

When you communicate with people, it's crucial to focus on their reception and processing of information, as previously described. However, this can become challenging in a larger group, especially with diverse type present. There are, however, simple aspects you can consider in order to appear convincing even in front of a larger group For instance, if you're giving a presentation at a trade fair or in a larger meeting, it's important to speak slowly, use shortened sentences, and pause between them. You should also ensure that your audience understands what you're saying and where you are at all times. A clear structure that makes this evident can help. Your opening statement should consist of ideas that everyone listening can agree with. This will capture their attention and create common ground. Additionally, emphasis is your friend. If you believe that a particular statement will face resistance, you can pose it as a question. You should also clearly highlight opposing concepts to make the polarization clear to your audience. (Prost, 2010, p. 79)

Example

You are presenting to your department with an audience of approximately 20 people. Since you are aware that everyone in attendance possesses a certain level of knowledge regarding the subject, it is acceptable to use common technical terms. However, it is important to ensure that you speak slowly and clearly so that everyone can understand you. To organize your presentation, you have divided it into several subheadings so that your colleagues can easily relate to the company and your department. At the beginning of your presentation, you provide a brief summary of the key points your colleagues need to understand in order to follow your presentation. This gives you two advantages: Firstly, it serves as an appropriate introduction because it reinforces existing knowledge that your colleagues can readily agree with. Secondly, the summary serves as a reminder of the necessary knowledge for your colleagues to follow your presentation effectively.

If you want to convince someone, this person must also know that your message is about them. The best way to achieve this is by addressing them directly. It common for people to talk about their own opinions, experiences, and thoughts during a conversation, but if your goal is to convince someone, you should avoid this because the other person is more interested in themselves than in you. Therefore, address them directly as much as possible, using their name if you are in a smaller group, or „you" if you are speaking to a larger audience. By doing so, you can create a connection with your audience and convey your message more effectively. When addressing your audience, focus on them and talk about yourself less. Towards the end of your presentation, you can use „we." However, it is important to avoid using „we" too early because it implies that you and your listeners have something in common, which may not be the case. Even if you have a common goal or interest, most of your audience will not feel that way until the end. The sense of community emerges only during the course of your speech or talk, so you can transition from „you" and „I" to „we" at the end. For longer speeches or presentations, a good rule of thumb is to use „you" for 80% of your speech, „I" for about 15%, and „we" for only 5%. Therefore, emphasize „you" first and foremost, then include „I" to a lesser extent, and conclude with „we." (Ibid. pp. 81-82)

Example

During a meeting where everyone present is expected to present a measure for improving the social climate in the company, one of your colleagues starts the meeting and immediately begins talking only about himself: „My suggestion is measure XY. I think that ... I talked to a few colleagues and found out that ..." After just a few minutes, you stop listening to him because it's not interesting to listen to someone who only talks about himself. When it's your turn to present, you make sure to include your colleagues in your talk: „I'm sure you've noticed that communication in the company has been a little bumpy in recent weeks and months. One measure that could help improve this is to introduce another form of communication in addition to e-mails. This would allow you to choose when to send or reply to a message. In my experience, this form of self-organization brings more freedom and also reduces stress. Ultimately, our goal is for all of us to be satisfied with our workplace."

In this example, you first saw how things should not be done and then how a well-distributed approach to speeches can make a difference. You may have noticed that the second speech had a greater impact.

Not only is the salutation relevant to getting the attention of your audience, but you also want to motivate them to take action and do something they haven't done before. One effective way to do this is to address a person's basic motives and needs, which can be categorized as physical or psychological. Physical needs are biological, such as the need to eat, drink, and sleep to survive. Psychological needs, on the other hand, include recognition, happiness, and security. If you can tap into these needs, you can easily get your audience on your side. You don't necessarily have to promise the fulfillment of these needs to appeal to your audience because it can work the other way around too. You can give the impression that a basic need has not been met or that it is being threatened. Alternatively, you can suggest that your audience must take specific actions to protect themselves or gain an advantage. It doesn't matter which approach you choose, as long as you can convey the idea that your audience needs to take action. To do this, you only need to trigger a single basic need and focus on it intensively. (Ibid. p. 83)

Example

You are giving a presentation at a trade show about nutrition, and you want to persuade your audience to consider healthier eating habits.

You: „How was your breakfast this morning, and how long ago did you eat it? We all have individual nutritional needs, but we all get hungry and require the right nutrients to fuel our day. My goal is to show you how to easily incorporate healthy eating habits into your daily routine."

By acknowledging the basic need for sustenance and highlighting the importance of proper nutrition, you have captured the attention of your listeners. They are now more likely to engage with your presentation and consider your message about healthier eating habits.

How to Convince with Your Personality

Conviction is closely linked to your personality. On the one hand, you must truly believe in what you present to others, but on the other hand, you won't be successful if you can't confidently and authentically express your personality. To develop your personality and use it effectively to convince others, we will explore the various levels on which personality is expressed and how you can leverage them to better persuade people and improve your personality. We will closely examine your personality and provide guidance on what is involved in developing a convincing personality and how to achieve it.

How Your Personality Expresses Itself

There are seven levels on which your personality expresses itself. The first level is your life energy, which holds your identity and drives you to live your life. Active actions stem from this level. The second level consists of drives and needs, which are your basic motivations to act and behave. The third level is the level of character, which includes everything that has shaped you in the past, such as beliefs, values, and attitudes toward life. This structure allows you to experience emotions, which is the focus of the fourth level. These emotions also form the basis for all social relationships in your life. The fifth level is the level of intentions, where you express yourself in interaction with your environment and strive to actively influence it by seeking knowledge about the world. This leads to the sixth level, the level of reason, where you develop your sense of reality and imagination, your knowledge of the world, and ways to apply it. Finally, the seventh level is that of the mind, which is the meta-level where you find self-awareness, reflect on your actions, and evaluate yourself. This includes recognizing which parts of your behavior come from instincts or social conditioning and reflecting on them. (Prost, 2010, pp. 32-33)

Example

You have decided to build the habit of exercising in the morning before work. This habit is expressed through all the different levels of your personality, but each level manifests itself in a different way. At the level of life energy, exercising gives you the opportunity to feel proud of yourself and integrate that feeling into your identity. On the level of needs, you fulfill the urge to move and relieve stress by exercising regularly. Through regular exercise, your character changes in the long term, as you become more disciplined. On the level of emotions, you experience more satisfaction because you regularly achieve a goal you have set for yourself (level five). On level six, your reason tells you that you are doing the right thing, which further enhances your satisfaction. Finally, at the last level, you reflect on how you exercise, which helps you improve regularly, and this level also finds expression in your habit of exercising regularly.

All seven levels of personality come with the need to express themselves, and this expression can take on many different forms. As shown in the example, the expression of these levels can sometimes be contradictory or opposed to each other, due to their complexity. This can lead to inner conflicts, which, combined with outer conflicts, can drain your energy. You can improve your persuasiveness by resolving these inner and outer conflicts or, at the very least, learn to accept them (especially outer conflicts that are beyond your control often cannot be resolved). By doing so, you will radiate more harmony and credibility, which will greatly help to convince other people of your worth. (Ibid.)

You can use the knowledge of the seven levels of personality to improve your presentations and speeches. The first step is to establish trust with your audience by showing that you understand their needs and want to help them. By doing this, you can address all levels of personality. The first level deals with the self, and to reach it, you need to ensure that your audience can identify with what you're saying. Show empathy and compassion to make your listeners feel understood, which can help them open up and receive your message. The second level is about needs and drives, so be sure to think beforehand about the needs of the people listening to you. What drives them? The third level expresses character, and by showing that you have integrity and are authentic, you can connect with your listeners on a deeper level. The fourth level, which bundles emotions, is easier to stimulate. namely, by making people feel good. Make your audience feel good by creating a positive atmosphere. To do this, you should always be friendly and approachable and be mindful of your body language. Now that you've gotten past people's values and emotions, it's time to move on to goals. Think about your listeners' goals and interests, and connect your key messages with those interests and goals. This addresses the fifth level, which is about intention. If you're not sure what their goals are, simply ask. This shows that you are genuinely interested in the people listening to you. On the other hand, it is easier to explain to people exactly what you want to say. To reach the sixth level, everything you say must be well understood. Make sure that everything you say is easy to understand, and avoid repeating yourself too often. If you think your listeners don't understand something, ask for feedback. Finally, to address the seventh level of personality, you must intrigue your audience to the point where they think and reflect on what you're saying. By doing so, you can leave a lasting impression and make your message stick in their minds. (Ibid. p. 33-34)

Example

You are giving a presentation to your colleagues about a project you have just started. You want to present your plan and gain support and collaboration from as many colleagues as possible. To achieve this, you have thought in advance about how to address all seven levels of personality. You no longer need to address the first level, which is the question of trust, because all your colleagues have known you for some time. Even if you are not friends with all of them, there is at least a professional basis of trust with all of them.

Level 1: To address the level of self, you explain the guidelines of your project in a way that everyone can understand. You also present it vividly so that your colleagues can relate to it well.

Level 2: This level involves needs. Therefore, you need to consider the needs of your colleagues. Most people crave attention and recognition. So, talk about the team dynamics you want to achieve and how you will make it happen. Regular goals and milestones are an excellent way to distribute recognition.

Level 3: This level deals with fundamental values. You address what is important to you personally and what you want to implement in the project or pay attention to. What values do you hold? If you value a good balance in the project more than getting everything done quickly, you can mention that here.

Level 4: This level involves emotions. To win your audience over, you need to create a strong, intense image of success in the project! Paint a picture of what the last days will be like when everything is done and how it will feel to enjoy the success. The more intense the scene is, the better because the more your colleagues will feel with you.

Level 5: After evoking emotions, you may have already won over many of your colleagues, but it may not be enough to convince everyone. This is where the final levels come into play. Level 5 focuses on goals and intentions. You need to identify the goals of your colleagues. Although everyone shares the common goal of professional success, you must emphasize how your project can contribute to the success of the entire organization. By presenting a clear picture of the positive impact your project can have, your audience can infer the benefits of working with you.

Level 6: This level is all about comprehension and reasoning, and it is relatively easy to achieve. It is essential to ensure that your listeners understand your message thoroughly. Therefore, avoid complex expressions and refrain from repeating the same information repeatedly. However, it is acceptable to repeat a critical point if it is essential to your argument.

Level 7: The seventh level is the most exciting level, and it requires you to leave a lasting impression on your audience. Additionally, you need to highlight the complex areas of your project and encourage your colleagues to consider them. One helpful tip is to inform your audience at the beginning that you will be open to answering their questions at the end. By concluding your presentation by asking, „What questions do you have for me?" you can actively engage your colleagues and encourage them to think critically about your ideas. This approach not only ensures that your colleagues remember your presentation, but it also prompts them to think about your ideas and ask relevant questions.

Is Your Personality Convincing?

If you can master a variety of techniques to persuade others, you may make some headway. However, ultimately, it's your personality that will have a significant impact on your ability to convince others. So, what exactly makes up a convincing personality? A number of qualities contribute to this, including self-confidence, being at ease, and showing fearlessness.

Are You Confident?

The concept of self-assurance refers to both the self and security. „Self" has several meanings. On the one hand, it denotes the fact that self-assurance comes from within and does not rely on external factors. On the other hand, „self" also implies identification with one's own person. Therefore, the „self" in self-assurance expresses an internal aspect. The concept of certainty also plays a role in self-assurance. A fact is certain because it is indisputable, a source is certain because it is reliable, a plant is certain because it is stable, and a place is safe because it is free of hazards. These aspects transfer to self-assurance because it involves being certain of one's own strengths and relying on them. This also includes being internally stable and not posing a danger to oneself. (Ibid, p. 36-37)

Example

A colleague has approached you regarding the report you've written, and has provided some criticisms. However, the colleague's tone and language have been directed in a way that attempts to make you feel insecure. Despite this, you trust in your abilities and are confident that you've done an excellent job on the report. You have no doubts about yourself, as that would pose a risk to your confidence and well-being. As a result, you can calmly listen to the colleague's criticisms and respond to them without feeling directly irritated or insecure.

The objective now is to enhance your self-assurance by finding more security within yourself. It is important to realize that the self-confidence you seek is already within you. There are certain exercises and strategies that can assist you in achieving this goal. The first exercise involves creating a balance between your inner and outer self. This is a body-focused exercise that is great to start with. Begin by standing up straight and finding a posture where you feel 100 percent balanced. You'll know you've achieved this when you feel stable both internally and externally, without having to tense your muscles. This exercise doesn't require much strength, as your own stability is sufficient. If you encounter difficulty with this posture, start from your feet and work your way up your body until you find a balanced posture. (Ibid. pp. 39-41)

The next step towards greater self-confidence is relaxation, which can be achieved by creating free space. It's important to have free space in your life to work on personal development. All you need to accomplish this is relaxation and space. This doesn't refer to an actual physical location, but rather the opportunity and time to unwind and grow. The first step towards relaxation is being alone. Try to be alone without distractions or obligations, and let go of your thoughts while observing their direction. Initially, you may confront various tasks that you think need immediate attention. You can let them go, or ignore them if necessary. This exercise is akin to getting a good idea or inspiration while performing daily tasks such as showering. (Ibid. 42-43)

Now that you have learned how to create balance and relaxation, it's time to address a more challenging issue: anxiety. We will delve into this topic further in the next chapter, where we discuss emotions. Anxiety is a complex emotion that can manifest both in specific situations and over time. As a result, it significantly impacts your self-confidence, affecting you both mentally and physically. Anxiety can also inhibit your natural impulses, limiting your self-expression and confidence. However, fear isn't always a bad emotion since it can indicate that you need to react urgently to danger. However, in most cases, fear doesn't serve much purpose. It helps you avoid negative consequences from your surroundings, unconsciously preventing you from experiencing feelings of guilt or inferiority. Consequently, you make an effort to appear positive to others, but this often means you lose touch with your true self. The fundamental problem with fear is that it creates an expectation that you can't handle negative feedback. To overcome this fear, you must set your own standards for your life. Your self-confidence should not rely on what other people think or say about you. It's crucial that other people's rejection doesn't significantly impact your self-confidence. This approach isn't easy and requires mental effort to achieve. Alternatively, you can overcome fear in a situation by imagining the worst-case scenario and finding a solution to it.

If you have a solution for the worst-case scenario, anything else that happens afterward is either not that bad or something you can handle. By mentally preparing for the worst, you can calm down and regain your sense of security. (Ibid. p. 44-46)

Example

You quickly wrote the minutes of a meeting in the evening and handed them in to your boss. You have the impression that your report did not turn out well and that your boss will be very angry about it. So, you imagine that you will be asked to come to his office directly the next morning and he will explain to you in detail how bad your report is. But what is the worst that could happen? You will not be terminated because of a bad report. You may have to improve it or even rewrite it, and therefore lose an hour or two of work time that day. However, this work time can be made up. So, your worst-case scenario is not as bad as your thought spiral. With this preparation, you can now calm down and face your boss confidently the next day.

Now that you've delved into self-confidence, you've learned how to create inner and outer balance, relax, and reduce fears. In the next section, we'll explore how to cultivate a positive self-image, which is also essential for projecting a convincing personality.

Your Self-Image – How Do You See Yourself?

Many people tend to judge themselves harshly. They form beliefs such as „I'm too impatient!" or „I just can't get organized!" which can be detrimental to their lives. Your self-image is the collection of all the beliefs you hold about yourself, both positive and negative. In reality, there are no inherently bad qualities, only those that are considered negative by society. To improve your self-image, you need to challenge your negative beliefs about yourself and find new evaluations for the qualities you previously thought were bad. For example, if you see yourself as too impatient, you can transform that into being energetic and active. If you sometimes feel fear, which you might consider bad, you can reframe it as caution. (Ibid. p. 55)

Your Clarity – Are You Sure?

On the previous pages, you learned a lot about personality and the different levels that make it up. Now, it's time to continue working with these levels. This will also contribute to your self-confidence, because how can you be self-confident if you don't know what is important to you? It's not just about committing to something; it's about finding what truly resonates with you. To do this, start at level 1 and find out who you really are! Everyone has a certain understanding of themselves, but it's important to push beyond that and ask deeper questions. What is your purpose? What kind of person do you want to be? What contribution do you want to make? Once you have a clearer idea of your identity, you can move on to level 2 and consider your needs. Knowing your needs can make life easier for yourself and those around you. By being clear about what you need, you can communicate more effectively and improve your relationships. To determine your needs, it's helpful to observe yourself and your experiences. This will lead you to your deeper motivations, which is the next level. After understanding your needs and motivations, you can explore your values. What are you guided by in life? Are you driven by a sense of justice or curiosity? Knowing your values gives you direction and purpose that you can't get from anything else. It makes you more self-aware and self-determined. Once you have a good understanding of your identity, needs, motivations, and values, you can move on to the final level, which is your feelings. Take the time to figure out what you're feeling, even if it's difficult. When you know your feelings, you can make better decisions and communicate more effectively with others. This can help you in many aspects of your life, from hobbies to friendships to professional relationships. Remember, if you want to persuade someone, it's important that they know how you feel, so it's important that you know it too. (Ibid. pp. 57-60)

The last three levels that you will be dealing with are your goals, opportunities, and the real choices. Your goals are the things that you want to achieve and focus your energy on. If these goals are clear to you, you will know exactly where you want to go and can live your life with relaxed clarity. To achieve these goals, you need to look at your opportunities and assess what is within your means and what is realistically achievable. You need to look at it objectively and determine what needs to be done to reach your goals. The final level is that of decision-making. If you have reached the end of your path to clarity, you have invested a lot of energy and thought intensively about yourself and your life. Now it's time to put all this investment to good use. At the final level, all you have to do is decide to take action and use what you have found out about yourself to achieve your goals. (Ibid. pp. 60-61)

Exercise for More Clarity

You now have the knowledge of how to gain clarity, and this exercise is designed to help you even further along the way. All you need for this exercise is something to write with. Use the individual levels as headings and find your clarity by formulating clearly what you discover about yourself for each level. This will assist you in organizing your thoughts so that you do not lose them again. Writing things down has the great advantage of compelling you to be precise and delve deeper than you would in a conversation. It is essential that you continue to work on it in a disciplined manner, even if it becomes uncomfortable, especially when it comes to deep-seated needs and emotions that may make you feel vulnerable. However, it is crucial for your clarity that you persist, taking regular breaks to maintain your concentration. If you can read everything coherently at the end, you will recognize the next impulses and the direction that will be right for you. Another aspect of this exercise is the flow of your thoughts. It is not necessary for all your thoughts to fit together logically. If you concentrate too much on writing coherently, you may suppress some thoughts, which is not recommended. In this exercise, trust your own thoughts, and let them guide you toward what you truly desire. (Ibid. pp. 61-62)

Summary

It takes a lot to be able to positively influence a person. You have learned many strategies for doing so in this chapter, and now you can use them to develop yourself. Persuading someone means that the person understands what you mean, believes in you, realizes that you understand them, and sees that your idea will benefit them. If you want to convince someone, you should avoid arguments and pay attention to your counterpart. Admit when you've made a mistake, and show concession by genuinely considering your opponent's point of view. To be truly persuasive, your counterpart should say „yes" as often as possible and should also have ample opportunity to talk. You can also make your counterpart believe that the idea being discussed came from him or her.

Your argumentation is also important to persuade others. There are different argumentation structures and types of arguments that can be persuasive in different ways. These include factual arguments, normative arguments, plausibility arguments, authority arguments, and indirect arguments. You can use these to your advantage. You have also learned how people process information, and you know that people can focus on eight different aspects: their gut feelings, judgments of others, what is achievable, what is to be avoided, a need, an opportunity, commonalities, or differences. Depending on what type of processing a person has, you can use different methods to persuade them effectively.

Of course, your rhetoric and personality are also essential for persuasion. You can also convince a group well if you use the right techniques. As you become more aware of your personality, you will find that this development also makes you more persuasive to others. You have learned about the seven levels on which personality expresses itself, and now you know how to use them to persuade your audience. Your personality also includes the qualities that make you persuasive: namely, self-confidence, self-image, and clarity. The bottom line is that you can best convince those around you if you know yourself well and use your full potential.

Third Pillar:
Understanding and Managing Emotions

Emotions have a significant impact on your life. Every day, at every moment, you experience some form of emotion. Initially, these emotions may seem uncontrollable, and you may think that you have to accept them as they are. However, it is possible to change this. You can learn how to influence your emotions and experience more positive emotions in your life. To begin with, you need to understand what emotions are and how they work. After that, you can focus on different positive emotions and their effects. Since negative emotions also play a big role in life, it's important to learn about them and how to influence and control them.

What's Behind Your Emotions?

Emotions have a significant impact on your life. Every day, at every moment, you experience some form of emotion. However, have you ever wondered about the science behind emotions? In psychology, emotions are defined as a reaction that involves the whole organism and consists of arousal, expression, and experience. (Myers, 2008, p. 548) Accordingly, emotions consist of several parts. Firstly, there is the subjective experience, where something changes in your perception or thoughts, causing you to feel a certain way. For instance, even if you haven't met a person you dislike, the mere thought of them may cause you to feel tense. Secondly, emotions involve various processes in the brain. Throughout your life, you develop your own evaluations, judgments, and subjective perceptions that significantly influence how emotions occur. When you experience something, you first evaluate it based on its meaning to you. You categorize your experiences, and your emotions follow from there. If you rate an event as good, you feel differently than if you rate it as bad. (Rothermund & Eder, 2011, pp. 168-170).

Example

You and your friend are walking through a park on a sunny day. While you are enjoying the warmth of the sun, your friend prefers to stay in the shade. When you ask him why he doesn't want to go out in the sun, he says, „I got a bad sunburn on my face a few weeks ago, I don't want that again." Because of this experience, your friend now perceives the sun differently.

In another situation, a small dog approaches you and your friend. You happily bend down to pet the dog, having had positive experiences with dogs in the past. However, your friend is hesitant and fearful of the dog potentially biting him, having had different experiences. Because of your different experiences and perceptions, you both use different evaluations to assess the situation, leading to different emotional responses toward the dog.

When you evaluate an event in terms of its impact, your brain does not simply rely on what you perceive. Other factors also come into play, but they may not be immediately noticeable because the entire process is subconscious. This means that the evaluation and subsequent emotional response occur automatically, without conscious effort or awareness. (Rothermund & Eder, 2011, pp. 168-170)

Example

You are attending a weekend training course to qualify for a promotion. After completing the first day, you have passed the initial exam with flying colors. Reflecting on the test, you feel extremely proud of your performance. However, you also consider that other factors may have contributed to your success. Did talking to a colleague beforehand help? Did glancing at the table next to you just before submitting your paper make a difference? Or were the questions easier than expected? As you ponder these possibilities, your emotions shift, and you begin to feel worse than before. Doubt creeps in, and your confidence wavers. Without realizing it, your reassessment of the situation has influenced your emotions.

This emotion that you experience also manifests in your body through changes in your autonomic nervous system. The autonomic nervous system is responsible for controlling reflexes and the functions of internal organs, and it functions unconsciously. (Aachen University Hospital, 2022) As a result, emotions cause changes in your body that are beyond your control. This happens because your body interprets emotions as signals to adapt to significant events in your life. These emotions manifest themselves through your facial expressions, body posture, and voice. Facial expressions are particularly important because research has shown that they can influence a person's emotions. However, facial expressions are highly dependent on the social context and social circle in which you are in, so you cannot always infer a person's emotional state from their facial expressions alone. (Ibid. pp. 170-172)

Example

As a child, you were bitten by a horse. Years later, while on a walk with your family, you encounter another horse. Even though it's not the same horse, you feel scared and start to experience physical symptoms such as a racing heart, sweating, and shallow breathing. You're prepared to run away if the danger increases. Your family can see the fear on your face and ask if everything is all right. Fortunately, the horse quickly passes by, and you calm down just as quickly. You can then explain to your family that you're okay.

The last factor that characterizes an emotion is motivation because every emotion includes the urge to do something. For example, when you feel afraid, you want to escape, and when you feel angry, you seek retaliation. The behavior sought in these situations has already been successful in the past and should work again. (Ibid. p. 174-175)

It's important to note that an emotion and a feeling are not the same thing. Although the word „feel" is often used to describe the sensation of an emotion, a feeling is only one aspect of an emotion. Other factors that make up an emotion have already been described. (Ibid. p. 166)

Now that you know exactly what an emotion is and what aspects belong to it, let's turn to positive emotions.

The Benefits of Feeling Good

Positive emotions are what people strive for at all times. It's obvious because no one wants to feel bad. But when you feel good, you don't just feel good; with those emotions come other benefits. This has been researched by Barbara L. Fredrickson, who believes that positive emotions not only indicate well-being but also create it. Additionally, positive emotions have an impact on a person's mental and physical health. Although various factors contribute to well-being, such as health or social relationships, positive emotions influence how others perceive these factors about you. Through her exploration of positive emotions, Fredrickson identified several facts that provide a boost to a person's well-being. You can relate to all of these facts yourself by recalling situations in the past when you felt really good. At that moment, you thought differently, and your mental boundaries expanded. When you feel good, you are more open to new things and pay more attention to new opportunities, which you are more likely to take advantage of. It logically follows that feeling good is crucial for personal development because it makes it easier to overcome obstacles and find new courage. Fredrickson also recognized that positive emotions mitigate negative emotions and promote both mental and physical resilience. Furthermore, she observed that after making the mental shift to focus more on positivity, there was a significant change in attitude toward life. If you think everything is too good to be possible, then the last point is especially relevant to you. Fredrickson discovered that every person can influence their attitude towards life, meaning that you don't have to accept your emotions but can decide what emotions you want to have in your life. (Jensen, 2013, pp. 39-41)

What are Positive Emotions?

The overall collection of all positive emotions is also known as satisfaction with life as a whole. Examples of positive emotions include gratitude, contentment, hope, love, and joy, some of which will be explained in further detail. (Müller, 2013, p. 8)

Gratitude

Everyone says „thank you," but usually just quickly and without much thought. Have you ever truly felt grateful in your life? The emotion of gratitude arises when you consciously acknowledge that you have received something, such as a favor or a thing. However, you can also be grateful for your circumstances or simply for your life. In this sense, gratitude is not just an emotion or activity, but part of a larger approach to life that recognizes and values the good in life and in the world. (Frey, 2016, p. 38)

Gratitude is associated with many benefits, most notably an increased sense of well-being. But of course, you don't just feel better when you show gratitude regularly. You are also more satisfied with your life and have better relationships - due to receiving more social support from others and displaying more open social behavior. Feeling better also has many other positive effects, such as having a more positive impact on others, sleeping better, and improving your mental health. Negative emotions and states are also affected: anxiety, stress, and depression are less prevalent in your life. Overall, gratitude contributes to greater life satisfaction. (Ibid. p. 44)

Therefore, gratitude has many benefits that are worth pursuing. On the one hand, you can receive more gratitude from other people by showing more selflessness and helping others, which will evoke more gratitude from them. You can also act as a role model for others. When you support and appreciate others, more gratitude will be shown to you in return. Another way is to foster trust between others, such as through coaching or mentoring. On the other hand, you can also incorporate gratitude into your life on your own by integrating it into your personality. To do this, you need to fulfill several conditions: you feel gratitude frequently and intensely, you are grateful to have others in your life, you focus on what is in your life and express your gratitude, and you are grateful for the good that is happening in the present moment. It is important to show gratitude not only to others but also to yourself. (Ibid. p. 38, p. 46)

Gratitude Exercise

There are practical exercises that you can do regularly to incorporate more gratitude into your life. One of them is to collect things for which you are grateful. This involves reflecting on everything that has happened in a day, week, month, or year, and collecting all the things you are happy about and grateful for. This exercise helps you develop more awareness of these things and become more grateful accordingly. To make this exercise more effective, it helps to develop a habit or ritual, such as doing it after you wake up or before you go to bed. (Ibid. p. 49)

Satisfaction

Are you satisfied? You have likely asked yourself this question at some point. However, the psychological meaning of contentment differs from colloquial satisfaction. While satisfaction is also used in colloquial language as a synonym for „happy," „fulfilled," or „balanced" (Duden, 2022h), satisfaction in psychology is measured by the extent to which a person's expectation before an action matches what he or she experiences afterward. The degree of satisfaction describes how satisfied the person is with the result of their own action and depends on the deviation between expectation and result. If the person expected to be happier with what they experienced, they are dissatisfied. However, if what is experienced is rated as equal to or better than the expectation, the person is satisfied with what they have experienced. Here, one must pay attention to the fact that both expectation and the rating of an experience are subjective and strongly depend on the person. (Veenhoven, 1991)

Example

You go to your boss with a colleague to discuss a new project. It is a big project, and you have set your sights on being in charge of it. Your boss has already made a decision and tells you that you are assigned to work on another project that is already underway. You cannot understand this decision and are disappointed. After the meeting, you talk to your colleague who has also been assigned to the other project.

Colleague: „So, are you satisfied?"

You shake your head and reply, „No way! I wanted to work on the new project, not the other one! Are you happy with the decision?"

Your colleague shrugs and nods, „Sure, why not? I just wanted to work on an interesting project, and that's what it is."

In this situation, there is a big difference in the level of satisfaction between you and your colleague because of the deviation between your expectation and the experience. You had a high expectation of being assigned to the new project, while your colleague had a more general expectation of working on an interesting project. As a result, you were more disappointed and less satisfied with the outcome, while your colleague was more satisfied because their expectation was met.

Hope

Another positive emotion that has a beneficial effect on your life is hope. This is a combination of confidence, optimism, expectation and looking to the future. It is the general attitude of trusting in the future and being optimistic to that end. At the same time, it is a positive expectation that someone has. (Duden, 2022d) Hope, then, is a positive emotion that focuses on the future. Hope arises when you are in a difficult situation and wish that this situation would be better. So, you act in a way that is consistent with your desire for improvement. (Blickhan, 2015, p. 58)

Joy

Joy is a positive emotion that you have experienced since your childhood. You may have felt joy when you got something sweet or when you were able to play with someone. This emotion is also related to feeling safe in a familiar environment. In such an environment, it becomes easier for you to make progress in your development, and you become more playful. By trying out new ways to act, you can build and acquire new skills, which in turn brings you more joy. (Ibid.)

Love

Like joy, love also arises in a safe environment, especially when you feel safe with a person. This means that you are certain that there is no danger from the person and that you do not have to pretend when that person is present. You build a natural connection with that person and, as with joy, you become playful and try new things. Love is also associated with pleasure, which is related to the hormones released in the body when you are in love. Love leads to two people trusting each other more and being more closely connected. This creates a sense of togetherness and community. You can observe this when you see couples holding hands on the street. It is a signal to everyone else that these two belong together. (Ibid.)

Not All is Well: Negative Emotions and How It Affects You

Of course, there are not only positive emotions in life. While one day you are really happy, the next day, something can happen that will make you angry or afraid. Negative emotions are part of life. Therefore, you must learn to deal with them and counteract them.

Trembling and Sweating - What Anxiety Is and How to Deal with It

Especially as a child, you were afraid of many things. Everything that was new was exciting and a little scary at the same time. That's perfectly normal because fear is a natural emotion that serves to make your life easier. You learned early on what to be afraid of. For example, if a car is driving toward you, you immediately become scared because your life is threatened. Fear, in this case, is that signal your brain gives your body to stay alive. There are many physical symptoms that occur with fear, such as a rapidly beating heart, trembling, or difficulty breathing. At that moment when the car is coming towards you, you immediately become alert, and your body shows that you are afraid. You breathe faster, your heart beats faster, and you tense up. You do this so that you are optimally prepared to either fight or flee. So, fear in itself is not a bad emotion because, in some situations, it is justified and useful. But there is also the fear that blocks you so that you can no longer act rationally and avoid danger. Both types of fear are needed in today's world only in a few situations. For most of your life, you are safe from anything that could threaten your life. Nevertheless, you know that you are afraid of conversations with important people, conflicts, and rejection. The emotion is the same, the situations are different. Since you classify these situations as dangerous, you become scared. This means that you have it in your own hands to influence your fear so that you no longer feel afraid in situations that do not pose a danger. (Merkle & Wolf, 2019, pp. 70-71)

Example

You visit the zoo with your partner and child and stop to observe a lion. Suddenly, the lion makes a sudden movement and everyone present is frightened. You also experience fear because you recognize that the lion could be a potential threat to your safety. Although you calm down quickly, you notice that your heart is still beating fast. This type of fear is rational because it serves to protect you from potential danger. However, do you also remember exam anxiety? Many people experience fear and anxiety before an important exam because they worry about the outcome and their abilities. This fear is usually unfounded because an exam is not a situation that poses a direct threat to your life.

In this example, fear arises on one hand due to the potential threat to one's life posed by the lion. On the other hand, there is the fear of failing the test, which is one of the most common fears because many people want to avoid making mistakes. If you experience this fear, it is important to recognize that mistakes are a natural part of being human, and it's okay to accept yourself even if you make them. The fear of making mistakes is often rooted in the belief that others will reject you if you make a mistake. The fear of rejection is another common fear, and people who have it will go to great lengths to avoid it. This often includes sacrificing attention, self-confidence, and personal needs to appease others. However, it's important to realize that you can still accept yourself even if others reject you, as rejection has no bearing on your worth or who you are as a person. (Ibid. pp. 78-80)

If you have any kind of fear, it is natural to want to overcome it. However, you should be careful not to use short-term strategies that are not effective in the long run. The following strategies, which you are about to learn, are not effective for overcoming anxiety because they make anxiety worse instead of helping you accept and work through it.

Next time you experience fear, avoid the urge to run away from it. While avoiding fear may provide relief in the short term, it can have a negative impact on your life in the long run. By avoiding unpleasant situations, you may miss out on new experiences and opportunities. For example, if you are afraid of meeting new people, you may never be able to make new friends or build new relationships. Moreover, avoiding fears often causes them to grow bigger and bigger over time, making them even more difficult to overcome. Confronting fears briefly is also not an effective strategy. Although it is often recommended, it can be dangerous because it is difficult to sustain the confrontation for a long time. If you flee the situation before the fear subsides, you may end up feeling even more anxious because you have exposed yourself to a lot of fear without experiencing a positive outcome. Another strategy that you should avoid is using food, drinks, or substances to deal with anxiety. While they may provide temporary relief, they can have a negative impact on your health and do not help you deal with anxiety in the long run. (Ibid. pp. 72-73)

Surely, you are familiar with the expression „painting the devil on the wall." It refers to a person who immediately assumes the worst and imagines all the bad things that can happen. This is a strategy you should strongly avoid. Assuming a negative scenario and then being prepared for it is not only incorrect, but it is also counterproductive. It creates tension and only fuels anxiety. The opposite of this strategy is to simply not deal with the fear at all but to distract yourself. While you are in a situation that causes anxiety, you may still rely on this strategy to get through such situations. However, once this strategy is not possible, you will feel even more anxious. Similarly, social support can also cause you to become dependent on this strategy. Social support means having other people with you as support so you don't have to deal with anxiety alone. However, there is another motivation here besides anxiety: when you are anxious, you appear vulnerable to others, and they are more supportive and attentive. Attention is a natural need that all people have, so it's essential that you don't amplify your own anxiety just to get more attention. On the other hand, there are people who deal with their anxiety by simply not showing it. After all, fear is considered bad by society, which is why many people do not express their fear but suppress it. This strategy is harmful because the physical symptoms of anxiety do not go away but remain, making this strategy unfeasible in the long run. Lastly, procrastination is another strategy you should not rely on. You may have put off a task you didn't want to do before. However, delaying something that is seen as dangerous is even worse because, even if it relieves you briefly, it will make you more anxious in the long run. (Ibid. pp. 74-76)

Now that you are aware of the strategies to avoid when feeling anxious, it is important to learn the strategies that can help you overcome your fears.

When experiencing fear, the first step is to identify the factors that contribute to it, which are the situation, your evaluation of the situation, and the resulting emotion. The situation encompasses everything happening around you, including the people present, the place, the time, the weather, and what triggers your fear. Your evaluation of the situation interprets it as if danger is imminent, leading to the resulting emotion of fear, which can manifest as tension, increased heart rate, and the urge to do something to alleviate the fear. After identifying these three factors, it is essential to question your perception of the situation and evaluate how likely it is that the feared outcome will actually occur. In most cases, the perceived danger is not life-threatening. However, even if it is, it is essential to act calmly and rationally. If it is not, consider how severe the outcome would be if your imagination became a reality. This perspective can help you gain a more realistic and rational understanding of the situation. Next, it is important to search for possible solutions to prepare for the situation and reduce anxiety. (Ibid. p. 82)

Example

You have written the final report on a project and your boss wants to discuss it with you. You become scared that your report was bad and your boss will criticize you. The first factor of your fear is the situation: your boss wants to talk to you. The second factor is your evaluation, where you automatically assume that you did something wrong. From this follows the third factor: your fear of being rejected by your boss. , you should consider how likely it is that your boss will criticize you. In this case, you have never been criticized by him before, and you have also prepared the report carefully. So, it's rather unlikely that your boss will criticize you. Nevertheless, it could happen, which is why it's important to prepare yourself for possible solutions. If your boss does criticize your report, you can ask him what specifically needs improvement and work to address those areas as soon as possible. It's also important to accept that you made a mistake because making mistakes is normal.

When You Get Angry

Another negative emotion that many people have to deal with is anger. When you get angry, you feel like you have a good reason to be - and that can be true. Nevertheless, it is not good for you to be angry all the time because excessive anger not only affects your relationships but also creates stress, which can negatively affect your physical and mental health. To better manage anger, you should first try to understand it. There are two common reasons why a person gets angry. On the one hand, a person may feel personally attacked. Another person may have said or done something that made the person feel hurt, personally attacked, or disrespected. This can make the person believe that the other person has bad intentions and wants to defend themselves. Everyone has a need for recognition and a desire to be liked by others, which is why many people feel attacked very quickly. They feel that their need for recognition has been violated and want to defend themselves.

On the other hand, a person may have the expectation that everyone around them must conform to their standards. They expect everything to go according to their ideas and become angry when those expectations are not met. It is common for people to have these demands, but they are usually not problematic unless they are highly developed. (Ibid. pp. 151-155)

Now that you know what to look for in everyday life to avoid anger, it's not enough to simply pay attention to what might trigger your anger. If you're the kind of person who places many demands on your environment, you should be aware that these demands may only increase your anger. To counter this, you can rephrase your demands as wishes. By doing so, you'll be disappointed when they don't come true instead of getting angry because of unfulfilled demands. Therefore, you should tone down your demands to make it impossible for you to get angry in the first place. Another way to avoid anger in the long run is through acceptance. If you accept yourself for who you are, you'll feel better about yourself and be more understanding of others when they make mistakes. Finally, incorporating exercise into your daily routine can help reduce the release of adrenaline that occurs when you get angry. Exercise also helps you relax, which is beneficial in managing anger. Not only is exercise good for your health, but it also helps with anger management. (Ibid. pp. 166-169)

However, once you realize that something is making you angry, you cannot avoid the anger but must address it instead. The first thing to do is to accept that you are angry and not judge yourself. Since anger is a habit, you can only overcome it by being understanding and considerate of yourself. Next, deal with your anger by doing something opposite: smile. Even though you are angry, by using different body language, you can make yourself relax, and the anger will fade away. Did you smile? Then remember that you are responsible for your own feelings, and you control what you feel. So you can relax and let the anger go. If you still find it difficult to control yourself, try to put yourself in the shoes of the person who caused you to feel angry. Think about why they acted the way they did and what their background might be. Try to show compassion for the other person, and you will see that this is very helpful in reducing the anger. At the same time, try to let go. Letting go means accepting a situation when something has changed. When you let go, you accept that something is happening that you didn't wish for but has occurred anyway. Letting go will make you feel calmer and more liberated no matter what is happening around you. Lastly, you can try to change the situation, but make sure that the desire to change the situation and the goal to accept it are not in opposition. So do not hold onto the desire to change what is happening for too long. Instead, it is better to accept the situation and use the energy you would otherwise have spent on anger elsewhere. (Ibid. pp. 161-166)

Example

You have decided to stop getting angry with your neighbor who makes loud noises every afternoon, even though you have already complained several times. But it's another afternoon, and after a busy day at work, you find yourself feeling angry once again towards the inconsiderate man next door. However, at that moment, you become aware that you are feeling angry. You take a deep breath and accept your feelings without blaming yourself. You then think of something else that makes you happy, like your family, and you automatically smile. You remember that you don't want your emotions to depend on other people, and so you try to let go of the anger. You consider complaining again to the neighbor or the property manager, but you don't want to deal with that right now. Instead, you choose to remain calm and relaxed, even if you cannot change the situation.

Targeting Your Emotions

You now have a good understanding of your own emotions, but you may not yet know how to directly influence them. Emotions often arise subconsciously, but you don't have to simply accept them as they come because you have the power to control what happens in your life. If you notice that you're experiencing an emotion that is not beneficial to you, then you should take action and not passively let it affect your life. What can you do?

Strategies to Manage Your Emotions

Your emotions arise in four stages: first, a situation occurs, to which you then direct your attention. You evaluate this situation according to the criteria you have acquired throughout your life in order to finally react to it. This is when the emotion occurs. The first strategy kicks in even before the situation itself. This is because you can select a specific situation, knowing from previous experiences how you will feel. If you want to feel good, you look for a situation that triggers positive emotions. However, if you cannot choose the situation, you should try to change it. This works both before and during the situation. For example, if you're particularly anxious before a lecture, you can ask a friend to sit in the front row so you have a familiar face in front of you. While you are in the situation, use your attention. Subconsciously, you decide what is important and what you can block out. You can increase or decrease the intensity of the emotion you feel by focusing your attention on different things. If you focus on the aspects that trigger the emotion, you will feel it more strongly. Conversely, if you focus on non-emotional stimuli, you will distract yourself and feel the emotion less. The most effective way to address your emotions is by accessing your subconscious mind. This is where you evaluate the situation, and your emotion is a direct result of this evaluation. Through repetition and targeted training, you can incorporate new evaluations and associations into your subconscious mind, which will enable you to automatically evaluate a new situation better. (Rothermund & Eder, 2011, pp. 199-200)

Most of the time, however, you only become aware of an emotional situation when you feel anger or fear. In the latter case, you can retrospectively think about the situation and calm yourself down, thereby regulating your emotions. Additionally, you can suppress your emotional reaction by trying to restrain your expression of the emotion as much as possible. It is crucial to take a long-term approach when dealing with troublesome emotions, as solutions that are only effective in the short term may not work in the long run or may even exacerbate the emotion. (Ibid. p. 201)

Example

You are on your way to an important meeting with a customer to win them over for your company. As you realize that you are feeling very excited, you decide to call a colleague beforehand to talk about the customer. This helps you feel less anxious because you feel more prepared for the meeting. Although the phone call provides some relief, you still imagine all the things that could go wrong during the meeting. To boost your confidence, you remind yourself of all the successful conversations you've had with customers in the past. Additionally, you question your own thoughts and emotions, trying to understand why you're reacting so strongly. You realize that you feel intimidated by the customer's importance, which makes you doubt your own abilities. However, you remind yourself that your boss chose you for this meeting, which means you have the necessary skills and expertise. You take a deep breath and exhale, facing the conversation with more optimism and less anxiety.

How to Talk to Yourself

Does it seem strange to talk to yourself? Actually, you already do. At any given moment when you are awake, you are talking to yourself, in your thoughts. Your thoughts significantly influence how you feel, but how you talk to yourself is individual. You learn it throughout life, and each of your experiences influences how you deal with yourself. If you have a problem worrying too much about what other people think of you or always being afraid, your thoughts are the first place to go to solve this problem. By actively taking responsibility for your thoughts and changing them, you can also influence your evaluations and no longer see yourself as a victim. Consequently, you are no longer dependent on other people or external circumstances, but you determine how you feel for yourself. If you say sentences to yourself like „This annoys me!" or „I'm afraid of this!", you can become aware of this and decide that you want to evaluate this situation differently to influence your feelings accordingly. (Merkle & Wolf, 2019, pp. 12-15)

Summary

Emotions are an important topic because they determine how you feel every day. However, you don't have to simply accept what you feel but can also influence it specifically. An emotion is not just a feeling but encompasses arousal, expression, and experience. It also involves the entire body. An emotion consists of several parts: the experience, the cognitive change, the physical change, the expression, and the motivation. Many emotions are classified as positive because feeling good has benefits. Positive emotions mainly affect mental growth and physical health. When you feel good, you are also more open to new things, take more chances, and feel fewer negative emotions. Positive emotions include gratitude (conscious recognition of something), satisfaction (matching experience with expectation), hope (optimism about the future), joy (safe trial and development), and love (safe companionship with another person). However, there are also negative emotions such as fear or anger. Fear is manifested by palpitations, trembling, sweating, breathing problems, etc., but many people are also afraid of rejection. To get rid of fear, you should not avoid it, but evaluate the situation, question your own evaluation, and then address the emotion. It is the same with anger. Anger arises from hurting or demanding too much from other people. To address anger, you should accept it, calm down, and try to show compassion. After that, you can let go of anger. You can apply all this knowledge about emotions by influencing your emotions. In this regard, there are five strategies: choose the situation, change the situation, influence your attention, change your subconscious evaluation, or suppress the emotional reaction and calm down. You also automatically influence your emotions through the conversations you have with yourself in your mind. So, be sure to eliminate negative thoughts as soon as they arise.

Fourth Pillar:
Breaking Toxic Cycles

Have you ever done something and then resolved to never do it again? Chances are you did it anyway. Most habits that are bad for you are a cycle that is difficult to break out of, but there are other cycles that you can encounter and harm: with yourself, with other people, and at work. All of these types of toxic cycles will be presented here so that you can get a comprehensive picture of them and defend yourself against them.

What are Toxic Cycles?

In order to shed light on the various types of toxic cycles, it is important to understand what a toxic cycle is in the first place. While the word „toxic" is often associated with medicine and describes something poisonous, it is increasingly being used in everyday language to refer to something malignant that poses a threat or causes harm. (Duden, 2022f) On the other hand, a cycle can be simply defined as a sequence of actions and events that repeat from a starting point. Therefore, a toxic cycle can be understood as a repeating sequence of events that harms or threatens an individual, and can originate from within oneself or be caused by others.

Your Emotional Cycles

There are also life cycles that we all experience, such as the cycle of fear. Many people fear negative reactions from those around them. This fear is natural, as they want to avoid feeling bad emotions like inferiority. However, they also fear being rejected by their environment, and as a result, they invest a lot of effort and energy in influencing how others perceive them, striving for a positive image. But this intense effort leads to uncertainty, as the environment only sees the side they have influenced. They may question whether their outward representation truly reflects who they are, and whether they can sustain it. As a result, they feel even more uncertain and fearful of negative reactions, which leads them to invest even more effort in their outward presentation. (Prost, 2010, p. 44)

Example

You meet with a customer to discuss an order for your company. You talk about the customer, your company, and the specific order they want to place. Suddenly, the customer becomes loudly upset about your company, how bad your customer service is, and starts insulting you. You feel responsible for this outburst of anger and try to calm the customer down, but they only become more agitated. You start feeling worse and worse, even though you know it's not your fault that the customer can't control their emotions. You start worrying about what other people would think about you now, whether the customer will continue to do business with your company, and whether your boss will blame you for the situation. However, you manage to respond confidently: You clearly tell the customer that you will not continue this conversation with them in this state and leave the meeting place. Although you have handled the situation well, you still find yourself holding yourself responsible for the customer's reactions.

Have you read the example and thought to yourself that you would have reacted similarly? Fighting these cycles is not easy, and it is okay to take time to do so. The key to these cycles lies in the experience or fear of rejection at that moment. If you believe that rejection is inherently bad and, therefore, you must prevent it at all costs, that is where you should start. As a self-determined person, you are allowed to set your own standards and decide whether the rejection of other people should influence you. If you manage to accept and like yourself, regardless of whether someone rejects you or not, you will no longer have to fear rejection. (Ibid. p. 45)

Do You Have a Narcissist in Your Environment?

Narcissism is a personality disorder characterized by individuals overestimating their abilities and achievements. They spend an excessive amount of time daydreaming about being successful, powerful, and attractive. Narcissistic individuals believe they are superior to others, and therefore demand special treatment and admiration. Although they are concerned about their image in the eyes of others, they lack the ability to understand what others want or need in life. This lack of empathy can lead to a condescending or disdainful attitude towards others. (Tasche, 2016, p. 42)

How do narcissistic people behave when they are with others? They want to assert their importance and demonstrate how great and infallible they are. If you have a narcissist in your environment, you will notice that it is important to them to be perceived as above average. To themselves, they are special, so they expect the same treatment from you. Living with a narcissist involves several toxic cycles that you should be aware of. In general, a narcissist tends to devalue other people to set themselves apart, keep others down, and highlight their weaknesses. They use the focus on others' weaknesses to avoid having to face their own. This behavior makes the people they criticize feel insecure and inferior. (Stahl, 2015, p. 127)

The toxic cycle that develops depends on both parties involved. One possibility is the strategy of valorization, which involves the narcissist idealizing the affected person to boast about having such a great person in their life. However, this idealization is often followed by devaluation, which pushes the affected person to strive for the love and affection the narcissist previously gave them. They may receive it, but only for a short time, which creates a cycle of emotional ups and downs that is very exhausting for the affected person. Another possibility is the strategy of endurance, used by the person who is dependent on the narcissist. This person makes an effort to endure the narcissist's criticisms and tries to meet their expectations. This effort is already toxic because a narcissist suffers from a distorted perception that is not affected by a change in behavior. The toxic cycle intensifies when the dependent person tries to live up to the narcissist's standards by becoming more beautiful or intelligent. However, the narcissist may still continue to criticize, causing the dependent person to feel they are to blame. Seeking recognition from the narcissist, and the subsequent lack of it, further reinforces their dependency and self-blame. (Ibid. pp. 127-129)

Example

You are sitting with your partner in the evening, talking about your day and what happened. Then your partner says, „You know, one of your eyebrows is much uglier than the other. It's really bumpy and straight." You feel hurt, but you don't want to upset your partner, so you don't say anything. Instead, you try to change the subject and ask about work. You continue talking for a few more minutes, but your partner comes back to your eyebrow: „Really, can you maybe fix your eyebrow? It's totally bothering me." You give in and go briefly fix your eyebrow in the bathroom, even though you don't think it's too straight or uneven yourself. „Do you like it better this way?" you ask when you return. Your partner nods briefly and then shrugs. Once again, you haven't been able to please them.

The example highlights the cycle triggered by a narcissistic person. However, toxic cycles are not limited to personal relationships, as they also exist in the professional environment. Let's discuss this aspect now.

Have You Experienced Toxic Communication?

Toxic cycles can manifest in the workplace and you may encounter a narcissistic individual there. Another example of a toxic cycle is paradoxical or contradictory communication, which we will now explore. A contradiction arises when you choose one option over another, thus resolving the contradiction. A paradox, on the other hand, cannot be resolved because all options presented are incompatible with each other. Communication is paradoxical when there is a verbal and nonverbal inconsistency or when multiple points are given that are mutually exclusive. When these two forms of communication are combined, it is called double-bind communication, and it creates a toxic cycle where a person receives a paradoxical instruction that can only be performed incorrectly due to the paradox. Consequently, they are accused of doing it wrong while the person who gave the instruction retains control and power over them. Additionally, an unwritten norm prohibits addressing this paradoxical circumstance. (Kutz, 2016, pp. 3-4)

Double-bind communication is a dangerous cycle that should be avoided. If you realize that you are already suffering from this cycle, seeking support is recommended. Addressing the problem is easier if you have others who can assist you. There are several strategies you can employ to combat contradictory and paradoxical communication within your sphere of influence. As an employee, you can demand clarification of unclear communication through direct conversations. Additionally, you can use rhetorical strategies such as humor and relativization to distance yourself from problematic individuals and take care of yourself by setting goals outside of this system and paying attention to other aspects of your life. These strategies also apply to leaders combating this type of communication, but they have more options available. In managerial positions, you have a greater sphere of influence, which allows you to actively influence communication in the company and establish authentic communication. This includes addressing and clarifying communication problems. A transparent and clear communication atmosphere provides a good foundation for communication that benefits all levels of the company equally. (Ibid. p. 41-42)

Example

One morning, your supervisor greets you and assigns you two tasks for the day. „Please do the update today, it's long overdue. Oh, and the report for the last project has to go out today too, finish that one too and forward it to me!" You realize that completing both tasks in one day is impossible. However, you also understand that your supervisor may reprimand you if you ask which task is more important or which one should be done first. To seek a solution, you turn to a colleague who has also faced this problem before. Together, you decide to confront your supervisor and request clear instructions.

The Cycles You Cause Yourself

You are familiar with your own cycles, such as when you make a commitment at the beginning of the week to go jogging every day, but then stop by Wednesday, only to feel guilty and repeat the same pattern the following Monday. You aspire to make jogging a routine, but in reality, it remains a habit of stopping and starting again. Or perhaps you experience daily stress after work and crave relaxation, leading you to drive to your favorite restaurant and order your favorite burger to go. However, this causes you even more stress, and the cycle continues the next day. Bad habits are the cycles that you are both responsible for and capable of solving. When you confront your negative habits, you will realize that you do not require external forces to overcome them. You possess this power on your own. However, let us first discuss what habits entail. Initially, a habit is an action that has become natural through repetition and consistency. After engaging in this behavior repeatedly, the sequence of actions occurs subconsciously. (Duden, 2022b)

A habit can be established either consciously or unconsciously. It begins when you consciously determine how to act in a given situation. You encounter numerous stimuli from your environment and learn what works best for you. Once you discover a suitable solution, you receive a reward: the correct response generates a sense of satisfaction. You strive to experience that feeling once again, so you endeavor to recreate the path that led to the reward. The more frequently you tread this path and attain the reward, the more automatic the entire process becomes. A habit develops, and you no longer need to make conscious decisions regarding that specific behavior in the future. This newly-formed habit conserves your energy, enabling you to concentrate on novel and significant matters at that moment. (Clear, 2018, pp. 36-37)

Example

You have started a new job and now have to commute along a new route to work. You decide to try a route recommended by your navigation system. However, on the first day of driving, you encounter a roadblock and arrive late for work. You realize that you cannot use this route again. The following day, you take a different route and reach your destination ten minutes early. You have enough time to grab a cup of coffee and chat with your new colleagues. You feel in control and satisfied. From that day onwards, you continue to take this route to work until it becomes an automatic routine. Consequently, you can now concentrate on other essential things, such as the day's work and meetings during the commute.

On the other hand, bad habits can develop in the same way. Imagine you go to a bar with some friends one evening. The ambiance is fantastic, and the drinks are top-notch. You have a lot of fun and agree to meet up again in two days. You automatically realize that you feel good in this bar with your friends, and you want to experience that feeling again as soon as possible. Consequently, you decide to meet up again and soon develop a habit of going out drinking with your friends. While this, in itself, is not a terrible thing, excessive alcohol consumption can be detrimental to your health. Additionally, you might not spend enough time with your partner on those days, and your sleep quality might suffer as well.

Do you have any bad habits in your life? You may not even be aware of them. One method that can help is to document exactly what you do throughout the day. For example, when you get up, go to the bathroom, make breakfast, etc. At the end of the day, you can examine your list and evaluate which habits are good or bad for you. You can recognize a bad habit when it seems good at first but has negative effects over a long period of time. Smoking is a well-known example: a cigarette may be relaxing and have a positive effect on your social life initially, but it is expensive and has very harmful effects on your health. (Ibid. pp. 52-53)

Now, the goal is to eliminate bad habits from your life. The first step is to identify the habit, which you have just done. The next step is to find out what triggers this habit. For instance, if you automatically reach for your phone and spend the next 30 minutes on social media upon seeing it, then your phone is the trigger. If you spend the first hour of your day reading all your emails, you can unsubscribe from the many newsletters you're subscribed to or turn off notifications from your email program. Once you have identified the trigger, you need to eliminate it. By doing so, you make the habit less visible in your life and lower the likelihood that you will follow the trigger again. (Ibid. pp. 75-76)

The second step to getting rid of disliked habits in your life is to find and change your associations with them. This is a difficult step that has a lot to do with your mindset and beliefs. You need to find out what you think about the habit because that's where you'll find what really motivates you to continue acting that way. You follow the trigger of a habit only because you expect to feel better in the end. When you identify what feeling you expect from a habit, you can effectively work to challenge and invalidate that belief. You can do this by becoming aware of the disadvantages that a particular habit has for you and all the positive things you will experience when you no longer have that habit in your life. Practically, you can go through your day mindfully and become aware of a bad habit before you do it. Then, repeat all the disadvantages you get from it and all the advantages you want to achieve. This helps you break the habit because the more you repeat these different aspects, the more you build the habit of believing them. So you are fighting a bad habit with a good habit. (Ibid. pp. 105-106)

The third step is much easier compared to the previous two, as it involves making it impossible to engage in the bad habit in the future. This means that there should be several steps or barriers between your current state and the habit, making it harder for you to act on the habit. To achieve this, you can use a self-commitment device, which is not a device but a decision you make to avoid bad habits and commit to good ones. This decision binds you to the good habits and makes it nearly impossible to follow the bad habit. For example, if you tend to overspend while shopping, you can decide to take only a specific amount of cash with you. If you find yourself wasting too much time on the internet, you can use software that only allows access to certain websites while blocking others. By taking this step, you are anticipating and protecting yourself from falling into the temptation of the bad habit. (Ibid. pp. 136-141)

Step four of breaking a bad habit is to build in a consequence that makes the habit immediately unsatisfying when you perform it. This consequence creates a barrier and effectively stops you from doing something you don't want to do. A useful way to make a habit really unpleasant is to have someone to whom you are accountable. You discuss beforehand what goals you want to achieve, what time period is involved, and what kind of consequence will follow if you don't achieve your goals. The person you are accountable to will motivate you to achieve your goals, not the consequence. For example, such a person may be your partner or a friend. The consequence can be an amount of money or something that is very important to you. (Ibid. pp. 163-164)

Example

You have a habit of staying up until at least midnight every night, even though you have to wake up before eight the next morning for work. Over the last few weeks, you've noticed the negative effects of this lack of sleep, such as feeling tired and less productive by lunchtime. Therefore, you've decided to take action to break this habit. Your first step is to identify the triggers that lead to this habit. After thinking about it, you realize that you spend too much time watching TV series and scrolling through social media in the evening, which keeps you from going to bed on time. To tackle this, you set an alarm for 10:30 pm to remind you to turn off your show. Next, you address your mindset. You recognize that you cherish your free time in the evenings, but you remind yourself of the negative consequences of not getting enough sleep, such as being less productive, patient, and potentially risking your job. Whenever the alarm goes off, you tell yourself that you would rather have good social relationships and a successful career than keep watching TV. The third step is to make it impossible to continue with this habit. Since you use the internet and your laptop to watch TV shows, you can either block your internet access or set up a block on your laptop after 10:30 pm. Finally, you make the habit unsatisfying by having an accountability partner who you pay five euros if you ignore your alarm and continue watching TV past 10:30 pm. By following these four steps, you find it easier to turn off your TV shows in the evening and go to sleep earlier. You have successfully broken your bad habit and established a new, healthier routine.

Summary

Toxic cycles are repetitive patterns of behavior that harm an individual. There are different types of toxic cycles, such as emotional cycles, like the cycle of fear. If someone is afraid of what others think of them, it's essential to realize that it's okay to be rejected by others. One can continue living their life according to their own standards and preferences. Another type of toxic cycle is when someone becomes a victim of narcissism from other people. A narcissist can make someone dependent on them by giving the illusion that the person is never good enough for them, causing them to continuously seek approval. Narcissism can also exist in the workplace through paradoxical and contradictory communication. These types of communication are characterized by the fact that it doesn't matter what one does; it's always wrong. There are various strategies one can use to counteract this type of communication, such as directly countering it with support while also distancing oneself from it. Additionally, toxic cycles can be self-inflicted, such as bad habits. A habit is a sequence of actions that someone has performed so many times that it happens subconsciously. To get rid of a bad habit, one needs to make it less visible, change their associations with the habit, and find ways to make it impossible and unsatisfying to perform. This involves building in lots of obstacles and accountability to ensure that the individual doesn't want to perform the habit anymore.

Conclusion

Positive psychology can have a tremendous impact on your life. In this book, you have studied the four main pillars of positive psychology and learned how to change your life for the better.

The first step you took was to focus on yourself: armed with knowledge of positive psychology and your personal well-being, you can now apply various strategies to become happier in your daily life. You can confidently tackle individual characteristics and relationships, as they also greatly influence your happiness.

In the second part, you learned how to positively influence others, argue effectively, and work on your own personality to become happier and more persuasive. This sets the right foundation for personal development.

Next, you dealt with emotions, a hot topic. You are now not only well-versed in positive emotions and how to influence them, but you also know how to defend yourself against negative emotions and become happier overall.

In part four, you examined what was holding you back: toxic cycles and bad habits. You can now identify and end various harmful cycles, including your own habits that you know are harmful.

Finally, the book provides the last impulse: be careful not to revert to your old ways. You now know about bad habits and must resist falling back into them. People often fall into habits, but don't let being your old self become one of them. With the knowledge you have gained from this book, you can make a lasting impact on your life. The biggest trap is that of comfort, which you must avoid falling into. Dare to make changes in your life. Be brave and show who you really are!

Afterword

Great job on finishing the book! You should definitely give yourself a pat on the back for taking the time to read and invest in yourself. In today's society, people are often too busy and stressed to focus on what really matters - themselves. But by taking a look at yourself, you have taken the first step towards living a happy and fulfilled life. You have proven to yourself that you know what is important and that you are the center of your life. Make yourself a priority and continue to develop yourself.

It's also important to note that this book has introduced you to psychology, which is a complex science that deals with the behavior, feelings, and actions of people. By learning about and understanding a subfield of psychology, you have expanded your knowledge and perspective.

Finally, it's crucial to apply what you have learned. You will only master what you know to the extent that you use it. Once you start taking action and really applying what you've learned, you'll immediately feel motivated. Active, inspired action holds so much potential that it can motivate you to move forward and make progress. So, allow yourself to be authentic and honest in your journey toward self-development! The best way to get there is by connecting with your inner self and continuing to grow.

Resources and Further Reading

Blickhan, D. (2015). Positive Psychology: A Handbook for Practice [Online]. Junfermann. http://sub-hh.ciando.com/book/?bok_id=1911979.

Carnegie, D. (2019). How to Win Friends and Influence People [11th ed.]. Fischer Paperback.

Clear, J. (2018). Atomic Habits: The Life-Changing Million Copy Bestseller [Online]. Random House.

Detlef Langermann (Ed.) (2004). Abiturwissen Literatur [Abitur Knowledge Literature]. Berlin, Mannheim, PAETEC Gesellschaft für Bildung und Technik mbH.

Duden (2022a). Bauchgefühl [Intuition]. Berlin, Bibliographisches Institut. Available at https://www.duden.de/rechtschreibung/Bauchgefuehl (accessed April 26, 2022).

Duden (2022b). Gewohnheit [Habit]. Berlin, Bibliographisches Institut. Available at https://www.duden.de/rechtschreibung/Gewohnheit (accessed May 3, 2022).

Duden (2022c). Glück [Happiness]. Berlin, Bibliographisches Institut. Available at https://www.duden.de/rechtschreibung/Glueck (accessed April 25, 2022).

Duden (2022d). Hoffnung [Hope]. Berlin, Bibliographisches Institut. Available at https://www.duden.de/rechtschreibung/Hoffnung (accessed April 25, 2022).

Duden (2022e). Humor [Humor]. Berlin, Bibliographisches Institut. Available at https://www.duden.de/rechtschreibung/Humor_Stimmung_Frohsinn (accessed May 6, 2022).

Duden (2022f). Toxisch [Toxic]. Berlin, Bibliographisches Institut. Available at https://www.duden.de/rechtschreibung/toxisch (accessed May 2, 2022).

Duden (2022g). Wohlbefinden [Well-being]. Berlin, Bibliographisches Institut. Available at https://www.duden.de/rechtschreibung/Wohlbefinden (accessed April 25, 2022).

Duden. (2022h). Zufriedenheit [Satisfaction]. Berlin, Bibliographisches Institut. Available at https://www.duden.de/rechtschreibung/Zufriedenheit (accessed April 25, 2022).

Frey, D. (Ed.). (2016). Psychology of Values: From Mindfulness to Moral Courage - Basic Knowledge from Psychology and Philosophy. Berlin, Heidelberg: Springer.

Hagedorn, J. E. (2013). Why Is Humor Important for Human and Organizational Well-being? In T. Möller (Ed.), Positive Psychology at Work: Developing, Promoting and Implementing Joy in Performance (pp. 77-84). Wiesbaden: Springer Gabler.

Helmin, L., Jakat, M., & Braun, O. L. (2019). Positive Psychology and Resilience Techniques. In O. L. Braun (Ed.), Positive Psychology, Skill Development, and Mental Toughness: Promoting Health, Motivation, and Performance (pp. 65-83). Berlin, Heidelberg: Springer Berlin Heidelberg.

Jensen, A.-L. (2013). How Do Positive Emotions Work? In T. Möller (Ed.), Positive Psychology at Work: Developing, Promoting and Implementing Joy in Performance (pp. 39-49). Wiesbaden: Springer Gabler.

Kutz, A. (2016). Toxic Communication as a Cause of Illness in Companies: The Double Bind Phenomenon - An Introduction for Managers, Consultants, Coaches [Online]. Wiesbaden: Springer. Available at http://www.springer.com/.

Merkle, R. & Wolf, D. (2019). Understanding Feelings, Managing Problems: An Instruction Manual for Emotions. Wiesbaden: PAL Verlagsgesellschaft GmbH; divibib GmbH.

Müller, F. (2013). „What is Happiness?" In T. Möller (Ed.), Positive Psychology at Work: Developing, Promoting and Implementing Joy in Performance (pp. 3-9). Wiesbaden: Springer Gabler.

Myers, D. G. (2008). Psychology: With 50 Tables; [+ Online Specials; Including Clinical Psychology, Industrial and Organizational Psychology, Educational Psychology; With Learning Objectives, Mnemonics, Exam Questions and German-English Glossary, 2nd ed. Heidelberg: Springer.

Preuß-Scheuerle, B. (2016) Communication Handbook: Convincing Appearance, Targeted Argumentation, Sovereign Reaction, 2nd ed.

Prost, W. (2010) Rhetoric and Personality: How to Appear Self-Confident and Charismatic, Wiesbaden, Gabler.

Rolfe, M. (2019) Positive Psychology and Organizational Resilience: Managing Stormy Times Better [Online], Berlin, Germany, Springer. Available at https://search.ebscohost.com/login.aspx?direct=true&scope=site&db=nlebk&db=nlabk&AN=1892088.

Rothermund, K. & Eder, A. B. (2011) General Psychology: Motivation and Emotion, Wiesbaden, VS Verlag.

Schmitz, B, Lang, J & Linten, J (Eds.) (2018) Psychology of the Art of Living: Positive Psychology of a Successful Life - State of Research and Practice, Berlin, Heidelberg, Springer.

Stahl, S. (2015) The Child in You Must Find Home: The Key to Solving (Almost) All Problems, 26th ed, Munich, Kailash.

Tasche, J. (2016). Body Psychotherapy Between Bioenergetics and Psychoanalysis: On the Interaction of Maturity and Vitality. Springer Fachmedien Wiesbaden GmbH. https://livivo.idm.oclc.org/login?url=https://ebookcentral.proquest.com/lib/zbmed-ebooks/detail.action?docID=4517730

University Hospital Aachen. (2022). Autonomic Nervous System [online]. University Hospital Aachen. https://www.ukaachen.de/kliniken-institute/ans-ambulanz/die-ans-ambulanz/autonomes-nervensystem/ (Accessed April 25, 2022).

Veenhoven, R. (1991). Is Happiness Relative?: Reflections on Happiness, Mood, and Satisfaction from a Psychological Perspective [Online]. Report Psychology, pp. 14-20. https://repub.eur.nl/pub/16151/ (Accessed April 25, 2022).

Printed in Great Britain
by Amazon

25036225R00069